HEAVEN

HEAVEN

Betty Malz

HODDER AND STOUGHTON
LONDON SYDNEY AUCKLAND TORONTO

British Library Cataloguing in Publication Data

Malz, Betty
  Heaven.
  1. Christian doctrine. Heaven
  I. Title
  236'.24

  ISBN 0-340-52434-0

This book is dedicated to
Sara Douglas

She has prayed for me 28 years, when I travel, when I speak, while I write, especially daily while writing this book, *Heaven*.

Sara celebrated Easter this year in the great Temple of Worship, east of His throne room, in the Holiest Place. She died the day before Easter. In God's overruling, practical, providential plan, she paid for the printing of a "reader's digest," mini-version of my personal resurrection story several weeks ago. We gave them to everyone who attended church Easter Sunday, while she lay in state at the funeral chapel two blocks from our morning worship service.

You spell Sara *o-t-h-e-r-s*. She called me that Saturday and asked, "What may I pray for?" I gave her the names of two men who were ill. She prayed for them on the phone, then closed by praying for the editing and publication of this book. Then, in her usual manner, she ended the conversation with a high, sweet *Bye*. She never wasted her time or yours.

Her last words were prayers for others and for this book. Her husband and our friend Lawrence called to tell us that she hung up the phone, sat down at the table, and fell over onto the floor.

The day of her funeral I took down from the top shelf of my kitchen cabinet a small glass decanter I have kept there for 21 years. It contains a dime and two badly corroded pennies. Explanation: That day 21 years ago I needed someone badly to pray with me. My husband had died following open heart surgery. My mother was terminal with cancer and my two-year-old daughter, April, had swallowed a dime and two pennies. X rays at Mease Hospital showed they were lodged in the sphincter muscle and after 22 days they still had not passed. April had a high fever, was very sick from infection resulting from the corrosion of the coins. Doctors decided to operate at 8 A.M. the morning of the twenty-third day. . . .

I called Sara to pray. "It's my birthday," I told her. "I can't bear the thought of my baby having surgery on my birthday."

She prayed, "Lord Jesus, our Great Physician, dislodge those corroded coins and cause them to pass." Before she said her usual quick *Bye*, she remarked to me, "You're going to have a happy birthday. It will be fun to see how God answers this prayer!" Two hours later the coins passed into the little white throne (potty chair). No surgery necessary!

She considered prayer "fun" and talked about heaven with simple, childlike delight.

Like Sara, we should learn all we can about heaven, even more than we would before making a trip to another country. After all, heaven is our future home—forever!

Acknowledgments

Ann McMath and Jane Campbell at Chosen Books
Ann, my editor and cheerleader
Jane, the "idea wizard"
Len LeSourd
Sharon and Lisa Huie
Bill Van Garven
Jennifer Stone
Ed Schlossmacher
Ed Tunkel
Roy "Chuck" Gates
Ethel Sipe
Karen Siddle
Debbie Daer
Paul Schurdell
Paul Priddy
Dwight Diller
Oden Hetrick
Elliot Hong
Charlie Messenger
Jack Cociloua (hair stylist)
E.L. Cole (portraitist)

Contents

1

Unrealistic Realities

It's not always easy to believe in something we cannot see. But unseen does not mean nonexistent. Scientists are ever searching the unexplored; children are born with a love for magic tricks; the middle-aged chase rainbows; the elderly hope to avoid the unavoidable—death. Every human has an inborn yen for the permanent, something lasting, eternal. It is the unexplainable hope of heaven and infinity. And that is the essence of faith.

But few things try our ability to believe in the unseeable the way heaven does. Heaven is the promise of all that is grand and glorious. It is the fulfillment of every dream. It is the place of everlasting joyful communion with our Lord Jesus Christ.

But we can't see it. We can hardly even imagine it. How can we know for certain, down deep in our hearts, that it is the most wonderful place in all creation, and that we as believers in Jesus Christ are headed there?

We learn about heaven most of all, naturally, from Scripture. The revelation given to John, for instance, gives us fascinating insight into the beautiful city, the New Jerusalem, and many events that will take place there. References throughout the Bible point to our ultimate destination and the lovely dwelling place of God.

We can learn in a corollary way about heaven from believers who have had near-death experiences and recovered with vivid recollections of what they saw there—although we have to exercise great caution and discernment about what we hear, always checking it against Scripture as our final authority.

I have enjoyed talking about heaven ever since my own experience with death, which I wrote about in *My Glimpse of Eternity*. After suffering a ruptured appendix eleven days before surgery—and gangrene, pneumonia, a bowel block, collapsed veins, and a coma—my pulse and heartbeat finally stopped. They removed the life-support systems, covered me with a sheet, and called my husband and parents.

I knew nothing of the happenings around my physical body during the next 28 minutes, for I felt as if I had gotten onto a roller coaster at Disney World. At the high point of the ride, the height of exhilaration, my body lurched with anticipation and I was launched from this planet to another. I was suddenly walking in a meadow of waving green grass among flowers of colors I cannot describe. I had arrived in the countryside of heaven. It was as real as England or America.

The gates were pearl as described in the book of Revelation, and I have never felt such belonging. Heaven is a reality! An unrealistic reality!

We can't see oxygen, but it is a necessary reality.

Our friend Clyde Miller, who pastors a church in Cincinnati, did a series of sermons on "unrealistic" realities such as those in the following list. These are things we have never seen, but would not deny are real. They are unseen, but they assuredly exist:

death	hate	life	health
energy	strength	fear	wind
peace	headaches	greed	depression
admiration	integrity	love	passion
faith	lust	joy	respect

The most *real* realities are the things of heaven. These shall endure while eternities roll. How important it is to set our affections on things above, not on things on the earth (Colossians 3:2).

Dr. Richard Eby, who recorded his "heavenly" experiences in his popular book *Caught Up into Paradise*, described his initial reactions at seeing heaven this way:

"I felt suddenly at home. I was instantly no longer in a strange world as earth had seemed so often of late, but in Paradise, personally prepared for my arrival. I didn't need my glasses to see ten inches or ten miles. . . . I had no memory of earth or the fact that I had plunged from an upper balcony . . . head first, with a thud onto the cement below . . . and was d.o.a. at the hospital. In a twinkling of an eye, as quick as a wink or a blink, my mind and body were renewed exquisitely beyond imagination.

"I gasped with glee at God and His handiwork everywhere in everything. I was home at last. What a joy! There was no pain, just a presence of peace. I looked at myself in a translucent flowing gown, pure white. . . . I viewed the forests . . . and the valley floors were gorgeous, with four-petaled flowers on stems two feet tall with real gold at the centers. . . .

"I looked for my wife. In the distance I heard her call, 'Richard, Richard!' The lights went out and I was on the fourth floor of the hospital."

Dr. Petti Wagner said that in her experience, even

though "I seemed to be walking on billowing white ether, there was a firmness under my feet as I moved. . . . I felt twenty again, uninhibited. . . . Human words cannot express the flood of emotions and sensations. . . ."

Personally, I have often wondered why God allowed me, a born again newspaper columnist born near Toad Hop, Indiana, former resident of North Dakota, now living in Florida, a second chance at life. I have never been to the Holy Land, but I think He may appoint me as a tour guide in the New Jerusalem since I've been *there!*

In fact, I have no idea why He allowed me to undergo the experience I did. Nevertheless I believe He has commissioned me and other "representatives of the resurrection" who have glimpsed the splendors of heaven to tell what is to come. We should "look not at the things which are seen, but at the things which are not seen; for the things which are seen are temporal, but the things which are not seen are eternal" (2 Corinthians 4:18). And the things that are eternal can be seen in this life only with the eyes of faith.

Remorse looks back, fear looks around, but faith looks up. When feelings fail, faith prevails. Our ultimate faith, of course, rests in Jesus Christ, who died on our behalf, rose again, and is in heaven now preparing a place for us. We know it is true because He said so (see John 14:3).

I chatted with a woman in the Tampa airport recently. She saw me reading my New Testament and remarked, "I'm a religious illiterate. For years I thought Joan of Ark was Noah's wife! But I know," she added more seriously, "that there's something after this life. I have never seen love, but I know it's real. I know there's a God, though I've never touched Him."

That's faith in "unrealistic" realities.

Job is a good example of faith in action. He was a respected and mature man. God said, "Consider him." When Job lost his possessions, his children, his health, he knew what it cost to hold onto faith. Even his wife suggested that he curse God and die so she could be freed from her misery. (What a miserable "helpmeet"!)

But Job persisted. He "reverenced the gap" between the things he understood and the things he did not. God did not reward him for suffering, but for holding on when he had no answers.

"Where is the place of understanding?" Job asked. "It is hidden from the eyes of all living. . . . God understands its way; and He knows its place. For He . . . sees everything under the heavens" (Job 28:20–21, 23–24).

And in this oldest book in the Bible, our friend Job—with neither Bible nor Christian books to draw from—nevertheless declared: "I know that my Redeemer lives . . . and after my skin has been destroyed, yet *in my flesh* I will see God" (Job 19:25–26, NIV, emphasis added).

We, too, must refuse to let things we do not understand rob us of what we believe. We must hold onto the hope of heaven and know that its unspeakable glories await us.

You may have a headstart in claiming this hope if you have had a loved one die. It gives us a personal connection or investment there.

An old minister friend of ours lives with his wife near the Wabash River. He said they used to sit each morning with cups of coffee and remark casually about happenings on the other side of that river. Then their last daughter got married and moved with her husband to that other side. Now they love to look out over the river because someone they love lives there.

The minister's feelings about heaven have changed, too. He used to preach funerals with some detachment. After three of his children died, however, he suddenly took great interest in heaven in anticipation of the time he will go there to join them.

To reach heaven ourselves we must first die, and that can be a frightening thought. We will talk about death more in the next chapter, but let's just say here that death is a reality we can understand only in part because most have only witnessed it, not experienced it. Yet with faith we can believe that death is the open door to the *best* of life—the infinite.

I have a hard time trying to picture that word *infinite*. A Princeton scientist, for example, says that the atom cannot be completely broken down. It is infinite endless energy. Another scientist says he believes in an immortal soul because science has proved that nothing can disintegrate into nothingness, so we ourselves must be immortal.

Assuming this is true, that we will live forever—which of course is what the Bible teaches—can create a hunger in believers for that eternal dwelling place. Reading the Bible can heighten our hope in the unseen reality of heaven. Realizing that Jesus lives there and we will walk in communion with Him is enough to burst our hearts with joy!

Do you have needs here? They will be met in heaven. Does your heart long for peace? reconciliation? truth? justice? All our longings will be fulfilled there in the light of Jesus' love.

In fact, there are many longings that can be met *only* in the reality of heaven. For instance, I will never forget the enormous sense of total fulfillment I felt as I walked along in that countryside toward the light of the city. The happiness I had enjoyed on earth compared to the happiness I felt in heaven was like comparing a forty-watt lightbulb to the sun.

I once interviewed a famous and successful writer. When our conversation moved to the topic of fulfillment he confessed, "I should be the happiest man alive. I have a good wife, five good children, darling grandchildren, and a contract for my next book. But I have a restlessness deep inside me."

"I know that feeling," I told him. "During the most important times of my life—on my wedding day, when I played my best organ recital, wrote my best column, lived my most shining hour—I had a corner of melancholy in the hidden recess of my soul that was still not quite satisfied."

During my death experience, while I was walking up that hill toward those gates, I was suddenly completely fulfilled. I was arriving at the place I had been programmed to go since the day I was born. I knew I could do things there I could never do on earth, or become what I had always longed to be.

I believe that the inability to find fulfillment in this life—the quality that makes fulfillment an unrealistic reality—acts as an anchor to forever, a bridge to eternity so that we will not settle down too comfortably here. St. Augustine referred to the restlessness in every human being for which rest is found only in God. Billy Graham refers to the God-sized vacuum inside every person. This tug helps us transfer our affections from the temporary, in which we desire the reality of fulfillment, to the permanent, in which that reality is found at last.

And this life is indeed temporary (2 Corinthians 5:1). Scripture says . . .

It is a story: "We spend our years as a tale that is told" (Psalm 90:9, kjv).

It is a pilgrimage: "We are sojourners before Thee, and tenants" (1 Chronicles 29:15).

It is short-lived: "My days [are as short] as handbreaths" (Psalm 39:5).

It is transient: "You are just a vapor that appears for a little while and then vanishes away" (James 4:14).

It is fragile: "He cometh forth like a flower, and is cut down" (Job 14:2, kjv).

It is ephemeral: "All flesh is grass, and . . . the grass withers" (Isaiah 40:6–7).

Our lives are brief, as is the memory of them in future generations. We can try to immortalize ourselves, but writing our names in earth's books is like writing them in the sand at the beach. The next tide will swoosh them away. To be perpetual they must be written on the permanent monuments in heaven. Just think: Your name was written in that unseen realm when you first chose to believe! "Every one who calls on the name of the Lord shall be saved" (Acts 2:21).

Even though our lives are short, we have enough time to meet Jesus. He said that if we believe in Him we will not die in our sins (John 8:24), and that our names will be written in the Book of Life in that unseen realm (see Philippians 4:3; Revelation 3:5; 20:15).

In the courtrooms of China are two books. When someone is tried and found innocent his name is written in the book of life. If he is found guilty his name is written in the book of death.

Similarly, every person here now on earth either has his name recorded in the Lamb's Book of Life, or he does not. Every person is heading for eternal joy with Jesus, or eternal damnation, separated from His presence and, thus, from everything good.

A niece wrote me about her stubborn uncle's refusal to believe in the reality of salvation or heaven. He was dying but had a miraculous recovery after believers prayed for him. His doctor teased him that "the guys with the horns came after you and I told them they couldn't have you!"

The uncle snorted, "I could believe in those streets of gold if I wanted to, but I think it's nonsense."

A dying man rarely lies.

Be honest in what you believe. Perhaps you are reading this and finding the reality of heaven hard to imagine. Or perhaps you think there is a heaven but you are not sure you are going there when you die.

Even if you cannot imagine the splendors of heaven, you can ensure your arrival there by believing in the One who paved the way for you. It is Jesus' home. Listen when He talks about it.

John 8:51 tells us that Jesus said, "If anyone keeps My word he shall never see death." What a bargain! We can be born again into a new life with Jesus. We can be assured that He has opened the way to heaven and is preparing a place just for us. We can cling to the unreal reality of heaven.

I have received letters from people in other countries of the world who do not have freedom of worship, even though they are allowed to attend church services run by the government. Yet these people rejoice that they have been born again by reading the Bible, a page torn from the Bible, or even a Gospel tract.

If you are a president, a movie star, or a peasant, you must experience both birth and death. But you can have victory over death by believing in Jesus (1 Corinthians 15:55–57). You can be assured of this not by the light of reason but by God's revelation. We receive the gift of faith poured into our hearts by the Holy Spirit (Romans 12:3).

I received a letter from a woman in Florida last year who told how she had been suffering from pneumonia. While in the hospital a nurse gave her a copy of my book *Angels Watching Over Me* and said she would pray for her that night when she got home. The woman said that during the night an angel came into her room and offered the strange message, "There is life, warmth, and breath." The woman believed immediately, put her faith in Jesus, experienced the new birth, and recovered her health quickly.

Most people, by contrast, have not seen the unreal realities we call angels; no one has ever seen the Holy Spirit. He is called the Comforter, the Prompter, the One called alongside to help.

This is particularly heartening in light of the fact that there are forces working against us, trying to cause us to lose our faith. The Bible says that Satan has made himself our prosecuting attorney. He is accusing you and me "before our God day and night" (Revelation 12:10; see also Zechariah 3:1–2).

But if we believe that Jesus died for us and that repentance of our sins means we are washed in the cleansing power of His blood, then we can consider Jesus to be our Advocate/Attorney before His Father, the Counselor for the Defense in heaven's courts. No wonder Isaiah calls Him Wonderful Counselor and the Prince of Peace!

Can you accept the reality of what the Bible says? If you have not already, please pray to Jesus and accept Him as your Savior. Make that reality a part of your life. Pause now and pray this prayer:

"Father, I know that all have sinned and come short of the glory of God [Romans 3:23]. I know too that the wages of sin is death but the free gift of God is eternal life through Jesus Christ our Lord [Romans 6:23].

"I now confess with my mouth that Jesus is Lord and believe in my heart that You raised Him from the dead [Romans 10:9]. By Your power and grace I claim that salvation is mine.

"Thank You, Jesus, for saving me. Holy Spirit, come dwell within my soul and mind and be my Teacher as I learn about the unreal realities of heaven, my forever home."

Many seem to feel that death is unAmerican. America is movie stars, sports, health clubs, youth, and wealth. But life after death is real. You did not choose to be born, but you can choose—and help others choose—to live a real life in heaven after this earth phase converts over to forever.

Vail, Colorado, is not heaven—even though there are no cemeteries there, and I saw one grocery store that displayed sixteen brands of caviar. Contrary to the belief of some, Clearwater Beach is not paradise either!

I suspect that many people—and churches, for that matter—don't witness to others because they are not convinced themselves of the awesome reality of the afterlife—

either heaven or hell. Are you married? You never answer that question, "I think so," or, "Perhaps." Regardless of emotions, you are either married or single. So with the question of being saved and going to heaven. It is so easy that some miss it. I've met people who are too smart to understand. But simplicity is the key.

Last night at bedtime I pulled a verse written on a card from our promise box of Scriptures. It was from Psalm 19:1: "The heavens declare the glory of God." Then I went to the sliding glass door in our bedroom and looked for the stars. I thought we were experiencing some fog outside since I could not see the sky clearly. Not until daylight when the sun came up did I realize our glass door was covered with dust from a windstorm. After washing it I could see out clearly.

Just so, we are to keep our hands clean and our hearts pure if we are to see the "unreal" reality of Jesus' love, saving grace, and eternal home.

Heaven is real, more real than anyplace you have ever been. And if you have accepted Jesus as your Savior, not only will you walk through those splendid gates one day, but each step you take is actually a step on the road to eternity.

Sound "unreal"? Undoubtedly! But as soon as we are willing to grasp the reality of heaven, we can start to consider that ultimate destination with joy and wonder.

We are bound to have a lot of questions along the way. For instance, will we recognize our loved ones? Will we have bodies? Will children who died on earth be adults in heaven? What about rewards and houses and recreation? By studying Scripture and listening to accounts from those who have had near-death experiences, I have come to believe that God delights in revealing to us some of the wonders awaiting us there.

I have interviewed 103 people who have either had a close encounter with death, or have died and returned to life, or have had a vision of heaven. They range in age from five years old to ninety-two. Our next chapter, "Death: Point of View," covers this vast age span, a full keyboard in its range and perspective. One need not be old to die or to contemplate the next life. I am amazed at the number of "printed-in-crayon" letters I receive from children.

As Spurgeon recommended, "Lay hold on eternal life. It is a thing of the future and it is a thing of the present."

Let's look at some of the answers that will help us "lay hold" of this unreal reality.

2

Death: Point of View

Arnold Toynbee, the British historian, has noted how Americans tend to say *pass on* or *pass away* instead of *die*. This gives the impression that we are trying to avoid death, even the mention of it. To some of us death is something to fear. To others it means oblivion, the end of life and the beginning of nothingness. To others it marks a time of reunion and celebration. To all of us it is inevitable.

Have you wondered what it will feel like to die? I read in a book by George Maloney, S. J., *The Everlasting Now* (1980), about the findings of two doctors who studied approximately a thousand cases of people at the point of death. They came up with an "average" description of what a prepared person experiences on his or her way out of life into what we know as death. This is what they wrote:

> When your heart stops and the hour of death comes, you will not break up and disintegrate like ice in the rapids of a river. Instead, it will be like diving into a new kind of reality. You will feel good and be happy in a very special way—"the peace which passeth all understanding." The weariness, the pain, and

the sadness all will be left with the sheets on the hospital bed. You will "light up from within" and then you will see someone warm and caring waiting to receive you. If your own close relatives are suitable for the task—and you for them—one will "pop in" as lifelike and loving as when you last saw him. But there will be a strange air of serenity around him. . . .

Something mild but powerful will envelop you. It will feel like the best moment of your life . . . you might have to grope for words—sacred, light, love. Neither one will really do, but you will feel it in the core of your being. . . .

The heartrending anguish of weeping relatives will appear to be childish and beside the point. Your own grand concerns—the unfulfilled dreams of the future, duties to loved ones, work, everything you ever looked forward to—will become small and unimportant, fading like dried flowers. With a sudden wave of joy, you will be ready to go.

My Aunt Gwen shares the point of view that death is nothing to be feared. She just turned seventy and concludes that an old body is like an old house: "After fifty it's just paint, scrape, and patch! The lucky ones are the ones already in heaven with all those repair bills behind them."

I asked my oldest daughter, Brenda, for her point of view. She is 35, married, and has two darling children. She told me:

"Years ago, as a little kid, I was frightened by death and heaven because they represented 'the end.' I was at the beginning point in my life with lots to look forward to. Papaw [her grandfather] would preach and say some peo-

ple couldn't wait to get to heaven. It made me wonder if
my wishing heaven could wait a little longer made me a
poor Christian.

"Yet history shows that revival—and a longing for the
life to come—usually accompany tough times like war and
depression. The pre-Civil War slaves, for instance,
couldn't wait for heaven because their lives were so miserable. John 3:16 says God loved the world. We should
look forward to heaven but love the journey, too."

My point of view about death has changed, too. Looking
back I remember more than once when I was about five
years old how my little brother Don and I would misbe-
have in church. Invariably Mother would whisper, "When
we get home I have a score to settle with you." In my child
heart I would pray, "Jesus, come quickly, before we get
home."

Later, as Don and I began to participate by singing in
church, playing his saxophone and my accordion, quoting
Scriptures, leading in prayer before the offering was taken
or to close a service, we paid attention. We were involved
and enjoying ourselves and eventually I stopped asking
Jesus to come quickly.

That desire changed once more after my own death experience. Even though I enjoy my life fully, I have an
inner longing to regain the fulfillment awaiting me there.

Circumstances can change our perceptions of death, as
can a newfound desire to experience heaven. I believe that
having anticipation for heaven is a healthy attitude, not an
escapist one. We are certainly meant to enjoy life, but as I
mentioned in the last chapter there is a fulfillment we can
find only in heaven.

Still, death is a curse and an enemy (1 Corinthians

15:26). So what point of view is best? Is death a friend or a foe?

A person's point of view about death depends on his understanding of it. Dr. Paul Walker and his wife, Carmelita, found her father's Bible shortly after his funeral. In the front he had written: "Death is the King's porter to usher in His guest." Do you think of death as the end of life or the fulfillment of it?

Jesus said, "Do not be afraid; I am the first and the last, and the living One; and I was dead, and behold, I am alive *forevermore*, and I have the keys of death and of Hades. . . . Because I live, you shall live also" (Revelation 1:17–18; John 14:19).

Each moment of Jesus' earthly life was a preparation for His death. For us, too, each choice made along life's way must be done with free spirit for the good pleasure of our Father (John 8:29).

Do you remember that Christ has conquered sin and death (Romans 8:2) and that it has no sting for the redeemed ones (1 Corinthians 15:55–57)?

In light of what Jesus has done for us, we do not have to fear death. Nor should we long for it, because our heavenly Father has a purpose for our lives that He wants to fulfill.

I prefer to think of death for the believer in Jesus Christ as a doorway with obedience on this side and fulfillment on the other. Here are eight aspects of the fulfillment I believe we will find by walking through that doorway.

First, death is a doorway into the end of suffering and pain.

A man in Mississippi mailed me a yellowed page torn from an old book containing the vision of the owner of a cotton plantation during his dying hours:

"I see a slave arrive on the shore of the river of life. He is met by joyous angels, and says, 'I cannot take it all in. It is too much for these eyes! On earth I had no window, not even a rug in my old cabin, no picture on my wall, no flower in the yard—*nor a yard*, for cotton growed clear up to the door. But I have everything here! Here I will sing in the choir. . . . You'll know us [slaves] in that choir. We be the voices that sing the most joyous and loudest!' "

I like that point of view. For those who are suffering death can be the door to joy and happiness.

Betty Pessaro had a grandmother from England dying with cancer whose husband had been an avid gardener. An aunt and Betty's mom were sitting up at night watching over her those last days. They heard a knock at the door, but no one was there. It happened a second and third time.

The following morning when her grandmother awoke, she said that she had spent the night in a garden so beautiful she could not even start to describe it. The family believes that her husband maintained that garden in heaven since he had enyoyed gardening so while here on earth.

I like that point of view, too. I think that the death of a believer is a door to the greatest peace he or she has ever known. My motto for life is: Anything worth doing is worth doing outdoors. (My husband, Carl, has a motto for life, too: Anything worth doing is worth doing fast! He says that when he gets to heaven he is going to spend forever in the library reading everything he didn't have time to read here.)

Second, death is a doorway to "professional" fulfillment.

If you love building, then materials, plans, and creative thinking await you. If you love farming, then you can count on crops with no bugs, weeds, pesticides, or droughts. I'm sure rose-growers will be busy, musicians working overtime. Nurses and doctors will undoubtedly have new professions.

Sharon Owens wrote to me from Lakewood, Colorado: "Last night I dreamed of my [deceased] dad. I asked, 'What are you doing up there?' He told me, 'We are preparing a place to your liking before we and the Lord come to get you.' He was in perfect health and told me, 'I have been doing a lot of welding, preparing the city.' "

Jesus was a carpenter and I believe that He will work with people in heaven as He did on earth.

Third, death is a doorway out of the reach of Satan.

I stand in the choir each Sunday morning at church beside Jennifer, who was thirteen when her daddy, Wellington Rose, died. He was an employee of Southern Railway and suffered a fatal heart attack.

Jennifer's mother told me later: "I stayed home with Jennifer while the pastor rushed my husband to the hospital. When Pastor Lowell pulled out of the driveway, I knelt and prayed. I felt a sudden burst of joy. I knew all was well."

The pastor explained: "Driving Beltway 495, I prayed for Wellington, then I fell quiet thinking about the joy of Easter near us on the calendar. . . . Suddenly I heard Wellington say, 'Father, I'm Your son,' then, 'Jesus, I've been wanting to see You.' He waved his hand in greeting, then slumped against me, dead. We were just a few minutes between the house and the hospital when it happened. There was an unexplainable, awesome power around us for about three seconds. It was not eerie, just strong and undeniable. It was like a tornado bottled up inside that car! Then it was gone. The doctor pronounced him dead upon arrival.

"Driving home I turned on the radio to hear Billy Graham preaching, telling how when Jesus came to earth angels accompanied Him through the 'principality zone of evil.' When Jesus died and returned to heaven, angels escorted Him back again through the atmosphere where Satan and his angels (the one-third cast out of heaven with him) reside. When a person dies, Satan will make a last attack on a soul that he is going to lose. At that moment God sends divine angelic forces to bring that person safely through that last attempt against his soul. He had brought Wellington on in victoriously. I could almost see the reception committee."

As we will discuss later, Bible scholars surmise there are three heavens: one, the atmosphere in which birds fly; two, space, which is occupied by the stars; and three, the heaven of heavens, God's eternal throne. It is the second of these that is considered to be the dwelling place of Satan, the "principality zone." The book of Jude (verse 9) tells how Michael the archangel contended with the devil over Moses' body when he died, saying, "The Lord rebuke thee." Michael defeated Satan and ascended through this same zone.

Fourth, death is a doorway into eternal joy.

When I was about eleven, my father pastored two small churches in Rosedale and Clinton, Indiana. It was Easter Sunday and on the way home, sitting in the back seat of the car with my smaller brothers, I said, "I don't want to go to heaven."

My dad almost wrecked the car. Turning around he said, "The pastor's daughter doesn't want to go to heaven?

You should not even talk like that in front of your little brothers."

I thought heaven was wall-to-wall church and I'd been born in church. We had revival meetings that lasted six to nine weeks, with not even Monday night or Saturday night off. Those were the days when pastors kept the visiting evangelists in their homes. When we had visiting preachers they used my bedroom and I slept on the couch or on a daybed in my brother's room. I kept a diary and one year I slept in my bed only 67 nights. I had been overexposed to people, church, and heavenly topics.

Another reason I didn't want to die and go to heaven was that one church I'd attended seemed to think you had to wait until you got to heaven to have any pleasure. This concept didn't appeal to me. I thought heaven was pale-faced people sitting on damp clouds playing harps. Weren't angels effeminate sissies with soft white hands and yellow curls? Or, like the Christmas card variety, fat, naked, dimpled babies playing sequined little harps?

It was not until my own death experience that I realized my perception of heaven's residents and the joy there was wrong. The angel who walked with me must have been seven feet tall with large capable hands and a masculine look. He could have been a bouncer or a bodyguard. People up there were having fun, building, working, getting on with real living. I arrived in the countryside (I'm a country person) but could see the awesome city with a golden boulevard down the center, a sort of main street. This city, the capital of the planet of paradise, was beautiful and appealing to me and I longed to explore it.

Which brings us to the next point.

*Fifth, death is a doorway to unimaginable travel and explora-
tion of the universe.*

As I walked toward those gates of pearl with my guard-
ian angel at my side, I realized we could travel just by
desire or wishing. Just as in our memories we can "travel"
back to another time and place simply by wanting to, so
we traveled at will.

If God's house is the universe and the earth but a foot-
stool in that immense house, then when we are with Him
we will probably have travel access to the rest of the starry
expanse as well. We will sweep through the universe as
the Creator's children, exploring crowded nebulae, packed
with orbs as thickly as the ocean beach is with sand.

Are these numberless worlds only lights in the firmament to illuminate our little world at night? They have
probably been prepared for habitation in God's eternal
future, places for the development and expansion of redeemed humanity.

Perhaps this will start during our Millennial reign with
Jesus. Revelation tells us that His servants shall serve Him
(22:3) and "shall reign forever and ever" (22:5) in the heavenly city, the headquarters of a vast universe.

Thinkers ask how we could travel up through space
without freezing to death. A country preacher I know put
it in these fanciful terms: "Elijah was transported bodily to
heaven, and he didn't turn to a block of ice on the way up.
No, the Lord took care of that! He sent along a chariot of
fire to keep Elijah warm all the way from here to glory.
You're thinking furthermore that as Elijah rode that chariot
of fire he could have been burned. No, God took care of
that, too. He sent along a whirlwind to air-condition Eli-

jah's chariot and keep him cool on his trip up yonder" (2 Kings 2:11).

The concept of travel in heaven has been described by a number of people who have revived after a death experience. Travel is as quick as thought. I found that by simply thinking of a place I could be there instantaneously.

This possibility of instant time travel is beginning to sound less and less fantastic to scientists. *Time* magazine ran an article in January 1989 describing "of all the strange ideas in physics, perhaps the strangest. . . ." It is known as the wormhole, and acts as a sort of time machine or tunnel that might be "narrower than an atom" and "vanish the instant it formed."

It would not seem at all unlikely to me that scientists could begin to prove some of the stories told about death and the heavens. I believe that a great deal of time in heaven will be spent exploring the universe and studying laws of science.

Sixth, death is a doorway into the greatest communications network in existence.

In Livingston, Montana, I met Andy Lundgren. At age five he had an interesting insight into this possibility. He had had a brief brush with death and he told me, "I went to a beautiful country. My grandma and grandpa met me there and introduced themselves. Since they had died before I was born, I wouldn't have known them. They showed me their beautiful house. One room had three king-sized beds and there were three or more big tables. The dinner was very good. Then they took me next door and showed me the house where my mother, dad, and I would be moving soon. My room was on the top floor where I could see the treetops, a pond, and a stream. In my room I had *two* television sets.

"Mostly while I was there I played outdoors with an angel. We played tag and hide-and-seek. He would disappear and then appear and laugh. The angel showed me a place close to God's throne; then I woke up. Now I know what to expect when I get old and go there."

The parents rejoiced at this report, by the way, because they had been deeply concerned about whether or not Andy's grandfather had received Jesus and eternal life before he died. They were comforted by this boy's unsolicited report.

My first reaction was, "Just like a kid to want not one, but two TV sets!" Then I received a letter from Len LeSourd that offered some insight on the little boy's vision and the communications network in heaven. He wrote: "Since not many of us have had the privilege like you to have had a glimpse into the next world, we have to use our imaginations somewhat to picture it. My imagination runs wild whenever I dwell on the subject. I see an incredible communications network that would make the biggest and greatest computer we have in our world today look like a child's toy."

That is particularly relevant in relation to a learning system I believe is in operation for infants and young children who arrive in heaven not having been instructed concerning Jesus' birth, death, and resurrection. If "there is nothing new under the sun" (Ecclesiastes 1:9), God merely renews and reviews for each new generation. One author suggests that dramas are presented in cinemas and on videos that people can take to their mansions in order to review the lives of Jesus, the martyrs, ancestors, and loved ones.

Ann Sandberg in *Seeing the Invisible* states that while "God is concerned with a great deal more than how many He can get into heaven, He is interested in numbers, for we read that in heaven the angels . . . rejoice over every additional sinner whose repentance they register" (Luke 15:10).

Are these events for rejoicing recorded on some sort of "computer" for review into eternity?

It seems conceivable that God may also have assigned some angels to "computers" that make entries of spiritual development. We are told that "they that feared the Lord spake often one to another: and the Lord hearkened, and heard it, and a book of remembrance was written before him for them that . . . thought upon his name" (Malachi 3:16, KJV). Could it be that records are kept of the individual Christian's progress? Is the Potter observing the vessel take shape and keeping a computerized video record the way a parent on earth would compile a scrapbook or photo album?

Seventh, death is a doorway out of the inequalities of life into perfect justice.

This could seem hard to believe in the face of so many trials that are hard to understand. I have a picture that was sent to me by a young mother in Loveland, Colorado. She had fastened her eighteen-month-old baby into her car seat in the back seat and begun a short drive.

Suddenly, at an intersection she felt a sickening *thud*. A man out on bond for drunk driving had rented a truck and, influenced by alcohol, had run the light. That mother picked herself up from the ditch and, to her horror, saw that the whole back seat of her car was gone. The baby was in the middle of the highway, badly injured. The little girl is now two years old. She just lies in her bed, eyes open, seemingly unconscious.

How can we comprehend something as "unfair" as this? Or other injustices we hear of such as honest people being cheated, good people being slandered, kind people being abused?

How can we comprehend other heartbreaking tragedies such as the one a missionary friend of ours suffered? He backed out of his driveway one morning not knowing that one of his children was playing behind the wheels of the car. The child was killed. Their other living child is severely retarded.

These families and many others who face the trauma of pain and heartache need our prayers and support. And they need to be reminded of the hope of heaven.

While there may be inequality and injustice in this life, there is only righteousness in heaven. Every action will be "proclaimed upon the housetops" (Luke 12:3) and that means that those who were wrongly or falsely accused will be vindicated. Everyone who has been hurt by the selfishness or rejection of others will revel in the love of Jesus. All wrongs will be righted. That young mother will find her daughter healthy and strong. The missionary and his wife will enjoy eternity with their fully restored children.

Looking back to my teens I recall that when the services at church would drag and people's attention seemed to wander, my father would call on another girl my age, Knoxie Crabtree (now Frost), and me to sing a duet. She played her guitar and I my accordion. We are probably much too "mature" to do this now, but then, young, in love with two men in the congregation, and of free spirit, we would sing joyously.

One of the songs we sang was called "I Would Not Miss It, Would You?" and it spoke of Jesus' return. One of the promises of His coming was that "wrongs are made right and forgiveness is sought."

Yes, there is a place where scores are settled and the books are balanced. But not here. After death we will find the justice we are seeking.

And, finally, death is a doorway that replaces fear with love.

A newspaper interview told the story of Augustine Chiedozie in Lagos, Nigeria. Augustine had died in a hospital in Aba on August 31, 1985. He had just finished a meal and appeared to have suffocated. He was dead for twelve hours.

Meanwhile, a doctor was reading the Bible before retiring and came across John 11:4, "This sickness is not unto death, but for the glory of God." He went to the hospital after dreaming that Augustine recovered and found that he had. The newspaper account showed a picture of the six nurses who had attended his body and prepared him for burial.

When Augustine came back he told them that the word *love* means "God." He arrived at this conclusion standing at the tail end of a long queue above a carpet of clouds: "I stood in line. A fierce-looking angel was manning a very narrow gate. There was an expansive table on which lay a massive book. I saw my name and four outstanding charges against me. Beside the book was a golden goblet of blood and a brush with a golden handle. The angel received a word from headquarters and stroked the blood across the charges four times.

"Suddenly the glory and splendor of music broke across the air waves and the trees and birds swayed to the rhythm of the joyous anthem."

Augustine was told to come back and tell what he saw. He was also told to serve humanity with love and without charge.

What should our point of view be about death? Perhaps one in which we trust Jesus completely, with no room for doubt or fear.

Last evening Carl and I sat on the upstairs sundeck of our little house here in Florida, feet propped up on the rail around the porch up among the treetops. We were laughing so loudly, my neighbor Robin looked our way from her car window to see what was happening over here. Let's have some fun at our own expense. This is what brought on the raucous laughter.

Carl said that when he dies he wants inscribed on the tombstone the words God said to Moses, "My presence shall go with thee and I will give thee *rest*." Then, to add some zest to the funeral, he suggested asking Lowell Lundstrom to sing his funny song, "U-Haul." The gist of the song is that you never see a hearse with a U-Haul trailer behind it. "You can't take it with you!"

I told Carl to save money, don't buy a coffin, bury me in my "green machine," the old 1962 MGA convertible I've driven so long. We both laughed at this since all my children want it when I go. Then, since I was writing this book about the afterlife, he couldn't resist saying, "Shall we bury the car nose-down to give you a headstart?"

I asked Carl to tell God, no telephones for me up there.

I would enjoy being buried beneath a palm tree, or being dumped into the ocean. I love the beach. Then I told him not to spend a lot of money on a tombstone. Take a piece of wood and with a purple crayon write, "I made it!" We laughed and the conversation got sillier.

Then we discussed our mothers-in-law. His mother, Rose Malz, was a big-framed German woman. My mother, Fern Burns Perkins, was a small-framed Scottish/English blend. They are both in heaven.

We visualized the two of them, sewing, sitting at a small, white, wrought-iron table on a lovely balcony with flowers below (they both liked flowers) looking down at the serenity of the flowing river discussing us, Carl and Betty, their children.

We could just hear Mrs. Malz: "Betty was lucky to get Carl. He could have done better." She sips her tea. "Betty was never missionary material. I know a hundred women who would have adjusted better to him."

To which my little mother retorts, "Poor baby. Betty is having a hard time adjusting. Carl is a man of strong preference. You can always tell a German, but you can't tell him much!"

They sip on rather than argue in heaven.

My first husband, John, is living in a waterfront home. Of this I am sure. He loved to water ski.

Carl and I could just see John chatting with Carl's first wife, Wanda, sitting on another balcony further down the river. They must have heard our mothers-in-law. The two of them really know us both and were laughing their heads off saying, "They deserve each other."

Of course, that was all made up in our imaginations, but it underscored for us the fact that death is not a fearful

subject. It is not something we discuss in reverent whis-
pers, as if we were unsure of our destination or unclear
about what we will find on the other side.

Do you fear death? I'd like to share with you an old
traditional family song passed down many generations. I
first heard it years ago when my grandparents sang it at
Lake Placid, Indiana, Camp Meeting U.S.A. My mother
had scribbled the words on some notebook paper before
she died and I have taken them with me on my many
moves from North Dakota to Florida to Texas back to the
Dakotas and now back to Florida again.

I took the paper out of my piano bench early this morning, played and sang it again. It has a lullaby rhythm and
soothing words. If you have any fears left about death,
perhaps it will minister to you as it has to so many others.
I can almost hear Mom Burns, my paternal grandma, hum-
ming it now:

A country where no stormcloud shadows deepen,
    Unending day, where night shall never be,
A land removed from sickness, pain, and sorrow.
    Oh, this is just what heaven means to me.

A place where there are no misunderstandings,
    Where from all enmity and strife we're free,
No unkind words, which wound the heart, are spoken.
    Oh, this is just what heaven means to me.

Where we shall see at last the face of Jesus,
    Before whose image other loves will flee.
And when they crown Him Lord of all I'll be there!
    Oh, this is just what heaven means to me.

Chorus:
What will it be when we get over yonder?
   And join that throng upon the glassy sea?
We'll meet our loved ones and crown Christ forever.
   Yes, this is just what heaven means to me!

It takes faith to believe that death is nothing to fear. It takes faith to get to that ultimate place of peace—heaven. The Bible tells us that without faith it is impossible to please God (Hebrews 11:6). But if we do believe, then our anticipation can be like an unseen hand that takes hold of us and leads us to that better country, through the doorway we call death.

Questions About Life in Heaven

One day not long ago I felt panicked that time was getting short to complete this book to meet my publisher's deadline. Yet my whole day was cut up like a tossed salad and my computer was constipated; nothing wanted to flow out! The phone rang. The doorbell rang and rang.

I finally put a red plastic sign on the doorknob: *Do not disturb. I am writing.* I heard a knock. Looking up I saw a large woman peeping through the window watching me. She called out, "Does this mean me?"

Before I could catch myself I retorted, "Only if you can read." Then, feeling guilty for being rude, I opened the door and lost an hour of time that I had wanted to spend working.

As soon as she left I skated toward the bookshelf to grab more paper and knocked off a large box containing all my foreign fan letters. I almost concluded they would lie there for the next two weeks, but then I picked up one or two and began to review the contents, the rejoicing and reports of miraculous heavenly thoughts. You read some of them in the last chapter.

As I read more of these letters from all parts of the world from people looking for Jesus to come back I realized suddenly how day-to-day worries were causing me to lose sight of the blessed hope: "Many shall come from the east and west, and shall sit down with Abraham, and Isaac, and Jacob, in the kingdom of heaven" (Matthew 8:11, KJV). That is the important thing, joining other believers in the heavenly Kingdom in order to worship God.

The questions about heaven asked in those letters are basically the same questions people ask about life. Suppose a family man contemplates a move to California or back home to Minnesota. Generally he sits down and concerns himself with six things:

1. Where will we live?
2. What will we eat?
3. What will we wear?
4. What about transportation?
5. What kind of work will we do?
6. What about the children?

Here is the way I would answer those questions—and others—as they relate to heaven.

1. Where will we live?

In mansions Jesus prepares (John 11:26; 14:2). We will live near Him close to His place.

Rebecca Springer told me of a vision she was given of heaven. She believes that many have a mountain home, a city home, a place by the river, or, for the farmer, a country home.

My cousin Pam's husband, David, said he would rather not go if he can't go fishing. My Uncle Bud is there now and I'm convinced he has a boat and is enjoying dinners of fresh-caught fish. The word *river* is mentioned 200 times in the Bible. I have not counted how many times the words *sea*, *stream*, and *ocean* are recorded, but it seems as though they are important in God's scheme of things and will be plentiful.

2. What will we eat?

Probably some fish, quail, fowl, manna, angel's food (whatever they eat), cakes, corn, and the bread of heaven. (See Psalm 78:24–28; 105:40.) I believe whatever God provided for the people of Israel in the journey through the wilderness He will provide in heaven—and better. God puts touches of heaven on earth. Every good and perfect gift sent down comes from God in heaven (James 1:17).

Two people who have died and returned to life wrote me of eating juicy pears from a tree that bears twelve kinds of fruits (which is mentioned in Revelation 22:2). Much is said about trees in the Bible. The same verse in Revelation talks about the leaves of the trees being used for the healing of the nations. I believe we will find vegetation and many fresh vegetables. We will have the ultimate connoisseur's taste and access to the satisfaction of those tastes!

To a child heaven would be candy. Italians may want lasagna. Greeks may prefer fêta cheese and seafood. Babies will want milk. Old folks may not be able to eat steak here, but I'm sure their teeth can tolerate it there, if there is meat.

In Canaan the land was flowing with milk and honey. The God who made Eden and so many fine foods here on earth will not shortchange us there.

A little fellow asked me a strange question. He wondered if there would be toilets there. My Aunt Pearl and I are nearly the same age. Mother's youngest sister, she was more like the sister I never had. As kids at my grandparents' country house in Indiana we used to sit in the outdoor toilet at night, gaze at the stars, and wish we could stay long enough on a trip to the outhouse so we wouldn't have to return ever again and waste our time. We preferred to spend our time playing. But it didn't work that way.

I suppose in heaven there is nothing wasted and, therefore, no waste material. Perhaps the little fellow was not so far off in asking that question. I guess God doesn't have to answer all our questions now. Some will have to wait. Deity reserves some crown rights!

3.   What will we wear?

The owner of a local boutique stopped me in the dressing room of her shop and asked me what they wore in heaven. There are many Scriptures that speak of robes. Oden Hetrick said he saw three garments. People were clothed in humility, righteousness, and garments of praise, three distinct layers.

The garment of humility was a soft undergarment. The next layer, the robe of righteousness, was very shiny, and the overlayer, the garment of praise, was a sleeveless coat or vest below the knee, beautiful and ornate, covered with precious stones.

He said he remembered most people barefoot. The children of Israel in the wilderness wore the same shoes for forty years, and they did not wear out on their walk to Canaan. I suppose God could provide holy soles to last forever if He so desired.

Robert Mosley tells the story about a Communist orator

who was holding forth in London's Trafalgar Square expounding upon the advantages of Communism. Alongside him, standing on another soapbox, was an evangelist telling of the glories of Jesus' saving grace and heaven.

An unshaven, unkempt derelict of a man was standing between the two soapboxes in the forefront of the crowd. The Communist spotted him, pointed his finger, and shouted, "Ladies and gentlemen, Communism can put a new suit on that man."

The evangelist responded by saying, "Ladies and gentlemen, God can put a new man in that suit."

Bobbie Morrison introduced me to her friend Norman Milley. In June 1976 he suffered a massive heart attack while living in Norwood, Massachusetts. They called his family together and he lingered in a coma for eight days.

During this time he was launched into the glory of God in another world. He says it is impossible to describe it in words. He met an angel who informed him that Jesus' blood had cleansed him from all sin (1 John 1:7).

He walked along the river of life, which flowed from under the city of God. Trees were lining the crystal flow. Another angel appeared to him, held out a gloriously white robe, and began to help him put it on.

He cried out, "Oh, please let me put it on!" The angel said, "First we must remove the robe that you now have on, for 'this corruptible must put on incorruption, and this mortal must put on immortality'" (see 1 Corinthians 15:53, KJV).

When Norman came to, the doctor was taking his blood pressure and he was crying out, "I want to put it on! I want to go. I want to take off this robe and put on the new one." They said he was tearing at his hospital gown, trying to replace it with an unseen garment.

He explained to the doctor what had happened to him, where he had been, and what he had seen. In four hours he was out of intensive care and improving remarkably. He has already lived ten extra years, and hasn't forgotten the wonder of that new robe.

4. What about transportation?

Isaiah speaks of seeing the King in His beauty and walking with God high in salvation along the climes of bliss. I love walking and this is all right with me, but the Scriptures also speak of many chariots of God up there. I have the written accounts of three who have died and who talk about chariots.

The vast size of heaven and the immense city will require good transportation, though we have forever to see it all. Since there is no hurry, chariots are furnished perhaps more for enjoyment than speed.

I estimate that they travel at least at the speed of sound and are propelled by the power of God, no motors, no fuel. The vehicles can travel over land, river, or sky. During my own death experience I found walking to be effortless uphill and down. It is more like a sensation of movement, like *being* more than *going*. And, as I mentioned in the last chapter, travel can also be as quick as thought.

It sounds exciting to me. The Scriptures bear out the facts that "in Thy presence is fulness of joy; in Thy right hand there are pleasures forever" (Psalm 16:11).

There is a strict man in my neighborhood who would be

uncomfortable there. He teaches the eleventh commandment, "Thou shalt have no fun on earth." Don't misunderstand me. I believe in the Bible basics. But a foundational principle is that heaven is a blissful Kingdom of great joy and—forgive the child's expression—fun.

5.   What kind of work will we do?

We will be set free from unrest. There will be no need to prove anything to anyone. We will no longer be prisoners of impressions or competition. But we will need employment for ultimate fulfillment, to make life most real to every individual personality.

My mother loved color and flowers and she loved to sew. I'm sure she is making drapes for my mansion and helping with the color schemes and interior decoration for the houses of my four brothers and their wives before we arrive.

She loved to visit us and rearrange our furniture. We used to get aggravated at her for doing this, but we let her. Then we changed things back after she left. God love her, I wouldn't wish her back to suffer cancer again, but if I had it to do over, I would accommodate her and others more.

I'm sure Aunt Lillian is painting. She was a gifted artist here. My two grandfathers, Dad Perky and Dad Burns, and my father-in-law Oscar Upchurch were contractors, carpenters, builders, roofers. They helped us build family homes and know what we like.

I still have the last hammer that my Uncle Leon Rogers worked with before he died. I'm sure, too, that God has upgraded his tools for heaven's kitchen cabinet patterns.

I laugh now remembering Dad Burns' eightieth birthday. He finished putting a roof on a house, came home at noon to eat his birthday cake with us grandchildren, and said, "I retire." He was an energetic man and I'm sure is gainfully employed hammering and nailing up there.

My friend Lawrence Douglas is only 82 and still tends his tangerine groves and rides his Appaloosa. He'll find plenty to do when he gets to heaven in all the fruit groves over on the hillside of glory.

Mom Perky, my paternal grandmama, loved to cook and give things away. I'm sure she's helping plan the menu for the Marriage Supper of Jesus and His Bride, the Church. My two aunts are like her. Each Thanksgiving I get a couple of packages from Aunt Shirley and Aunt Elsie. They mail me sage from Mom Perky's herb garden in Indiana, from her old home place, to spice up my stuffing for the turkey.

My first husband, John, died at age 36 following open heart surgery. The doctor gave him the option of not having surgery and slowing down his lifestyle. John chose the surgery. He said he would rather enjoy a short life than be bored and live twice as long. He was an achiever and motivator, winning awards from his company for volume business and new promotional ideas. John was also an outdoors person. This kind of person lives twice as long in half the time, completing his or her assignments here early. I'm sure that over there he is teaching people to water ski on the river of life.

Mom Burns, my maternal grandmama, was a different breed. She didn't fuss about housekeeping. She loved us kids and picking berries and making jam. We could jump up and down on the beds, ransack her attic, pour out the button box onto the floor and leave it, climb the cherry tree, jump onto the cows' backs from the cowshed roof, and bring pets into the living room. We never bothered or crowded her. I would bet she's rocking my baby brother up there until we all arrive.

I believe we will enjoy doing there whatever we enjoy doing here. There will be no toil, but joyful employment of all the powers of the soul.

If you are in agriculture you will enjoy your visits to the plains, valleys, hills, and mountains of splendor in paradise. If a teacher here, you may greatly relish instructing those who have just come from terrestrial shores to the eternal Kingdom. Those who are mechanics and engineers will find ample scope for expression there, helping the Lord prepare our mansions, employing the busy hands of millions of His saints in the most wonderful architecture of heaven.

We will look like ourselves and act like ourselves at our very best. Job said, remember, "And though after my skin worms destroy this body, yet *in my flesh* shall I see God" (19:26, KJV).

Luke 24:39 tells us that Jesus' resurrected body was intact: "See My hands and My feet, that it is I Myself; touch Me and see, for a spirit does not have flesh and bones as you see that I have." Jesus talked and ate with the disciples.

Yet in His resurrected body Jesus could pass through closed doors, appear, disappear, transport Himself from place to place, and finally ascend to heaven. When we go with Jesus to heaven we, too, will have glorified physical bodies like His (1 Thessalonians 4:16–17). "When He appears, we shall be like Him, because we shall see Him just as He is" (1 John 3:2).

Further, we will be known as we are known here. Let me quote again Jesus' words: "And I say to you, that many shall come from east and west, and recline at table with Abraham, and Isaac, and Jacob, in the kingdom of heaven" (Matthew 8:11). In other words, they will not have lost their identities.

6. What about the children?

The Bible speaks so much about children that that subject alone could fill an entire book. Children who die young are not unhappy being taken from us. There is no discontent or sorrow there, only supreme joy. No change of place or surroundings could make them happier, unless it would be to see their parents, brothers, sisters, or friends arrive, too. Then their cup of happiness will be full indeed. Be sure to prepare to meet them.

There are so many mothers and Sunday school teachers there who are loving the children. Jesus loves children. "Little ones to Him belong" are words from the first song we learn as babies. One man saw in a vision angels leaving heaven, going to earth to get children when they were dying.

In her vision of heaven Rebecca Springer reports that she saw the young daughter of a friend arrive in heaven and heard the mother pray, "O God, she is such a shy child and we have no one there to meet her or care for her when she arrives."

She came nestled lovingly in the Master's arms. He carried her, caressed her. She was sitting in His lap when a remarkably fine white Angora kitten, of which the child had been fond, ran across the grass and sprang into her lap. It purred, head under the child's chin, then lay contentedly sleeping in her lap.

The family had not been able to find the kitten since the child's death. Who but our loving Father would have thought of such a comfort for a little girl? She had been timid, but as other children gathered around her, she had delightful freedom manifested in Jesus' presence.

An angel in Rebecca's vision told her, "We have watched over you and others from your infancy. As a child on earth is instructed by a parent about heaven, so we teach children here about earth."

Our Father never forgets us and provides pleasures and comforts for us all according to our individual needs.

Perhaps this is why children seem to arrive in the garden paradise part of heaven instead of directly at the throne, so the shock won't be too great for them. They progress happily to the suburbs of heaven to play among the flowers and along the streams. If you want to know what heaven is like, read the Genesis account of Eden. The Bible tells us that God planted that Garden. That was, perhaps, a transplanted garden from heaven.

Dr. W. B. McCafferty says that old age is the mark of sickness and death. On the other hand, "older people will become youthful and infants will grow slowly and surely in the nurture of the wholesome atmosphere of heaven." They cannot get sick or be injured. And there is no aging or death there, or drugs or perversion. Indeed, there can be no sin at all in the dwelling place of God!

If a day is as a thousand years with God, I think that your child will not be a lot older than or much changed from when you lost him or her. Physically, as with our spiritual growth, God doesn't see me as I am, but as I'm going to be. You can be sure He has an ultimate growing up for your baby. There is no incompleteness in heaven. You can be sure as well that your preemie is complete, or that a miscarried child awaits you there. All of us will be in the springtime of our lives. The climate there is "forever spring"!

One born again Catholic nun told me that she believes she will mother children over there whose mothers didn't make it because of unbelief in Jesus. Some believe that aborted babies will be complete and that some loving women—perhaps those barren or unmarried on earth—will care for those children there.

One account of near-death records a conversation of child to mother: "It is better that I did not grow up down there in that world. I might have been a bad woman. God knew best." The parent later read Isaiah 57:1 (KJV), "The righteous is taken away from the evil to come," and felt it applied to her child's situation.

Marietta Davis claims she saw infants singing in a children's choir in her glimpse of heaven. They had lessons in music and singing and formed bands. They were also instructed about the birth, life, and death of Jesus. She said the children wore or carried beautiful flowers. In heaven's great worship Temple, they sat in small seats reserved for them by aid of a thousand golden chains set with diamonds and gems of rarest beauty.

I received this letter from a mother in Birch Run, Michigan:

> In 1980 I lost two of my three little girls in a car accident along with their grandpa, gramma, and three cousins. My daughters were six and eight. I cried out

to God, "I must know some way that they are in
heaven for sure."

It was a difficult task to go to their school to clean
out their little desks. In my eight-year-old's desk there
was only one paper. She had drawn a picture of her
and her younger sister holding hands going up into
the air to heaven, with wings, into a beautiful, colorful
sky. Immediately I had peace in my heart knowing
where they were.

Unless you lose someone very dear to you, I don't
think you really take so much interest in heaven. I
can't hear enough now.

People rarely believe in miracles until they need one. I
believe this is why God often shows us the way in life
through the faith of a simple, believing child, or an adult
with a child's faith.

This brings up an important point. Some ask if there is
contact with those in heaven. Make no mistake about it:
There is danger in trying to contact the dead. The Bible
strictly prohibits it as an occult practice. Don't try it. Talk
instead to God. Pour out your thoughts, worries, and fears
to Him and He will hear and help you, just as He helped
this mother. He alone is our heavenly Comforter, Guide,
and Friend. Pray to the Father in the name of Jesus, His
Son.

I should point out, however, that some, such as Sadhu
Sundar Singh, believe that on rare occasions God allows
us glimpses or impressions of our dead loved ones, perhaps in a dream or vision—such as some we have already
seen.

I told in *Prayers That Are Answered* how I was pregnant

with our second child when John died. April was born four months after her daddy's death.

At the hospital, when they brought her to me and laid her tiny little head on my arm, I wished John had lived long enough to see her just once, for a few minutes, even.

Suddenly in the doorway I caught a glimpse of white. Looking up, thinking a nurse was trying to get my attention, I saw John standing there. He flashed me a big, proud, boyish grin and was gone.

I don't know why God allowed me that experience. But I do know that I did not then, and would not now, seek it. If He chose to give me comfort in that manner I can only accept it with a grateful heart.

Perhaps you have other questions.

I have often wondered, for instance, if we would have knowledge in heaven of our lost loved ones, miss those friends and relatives who chose to live their lives without believing in Jesus and, thus, will spend eternity without Him.

Revelation 21:4 says, "He shall wipe away every tear." Our hearts will be full of the emotions of praise with no thought of weeping about anything. Our faculties and dispositions to sorrow or sadness will be gone, and we will see things as God sees them.

I believe people in heaven know what is happening here, but they are not depressed by sad events. They are in eternal bliss, happy with God's all-wise planning.

Hebrews 12:1, referring to prophets and martyrs and the believers who have gone on before us, says: "Wherefore seeing we [the living] also are compassed about with so great a cloud of witnesses . . . let us run with patience the race that is set before us" (KJV).

Roberts Lairdon said he saw a sports stadium, something like football bleachers, with many hosts of people in the stands sitting facing the outer perimeter of heaven looking down upon earth. They were cheering, standing, waving banners and flags rooting for us here while we witness, sing, and work for the Lord to win souls. They knelt to pray for us, he said, while some here were preaching.

Perhaps you have other questions. Have you ever wondered what language we will speak in heaven? No matter what language we spoke on earth, I'm sure we will fully understand each other there. Again, 1 John 3:2 says: "When He appears, we shall be like Him, because we shall see Him just as He is." He hears all the voices of the earth petitioning Him on the Lord's Day and is not confused at all. I personally feel that we will comprehend all the languages and be multilingual and speak and communicate with people of all nations and tongues. Many scholars feel we will speak the original language of Eden, the language that Adam and Eve spoke when they walked and talked with God. Remember that before the Tower of Babel, the world spoke one universal language? God confused their tongues because of their greed, competition, and pride. There will be none of that in heaven.

Will animals be in heaven?

I heard from one person who died who saw little children laughing, running hither and yon catching tiny birds in their hands, singing, playing with animals. Many have reported seeing countryside and plenty of space for animals. I feel sure they are not in the city section of the capital!

The Bible mentions a lot of animals. In the Millennium

the lion will lie down with the lamb. Much is written about horses and eagles. In Revelation 19:17 birds are told to come. And Acts 11:5–10 describes Peter's vision in which a great sheet is lowered from heaven with four-footed animals of the earth, wild beasts, crawling creatures, and birds.

I think these animals will be harmless and will have glorified personalities just as we will. For instance, the wolf and the lamb shall feed together and none will be hurt.

Will the soul of a pet survive the gates of death? God created animals in the Garden for Adam's pleasure and could resurrect them if He so desired. He makes the rules. It is impossible to say whether or not your animals will be there but of this I am sure: Nothing is impossible with God. If His plan for our happiness includes the survival of our pets, then they will most assuredly be there.

In fact, Rebecca Springer also saw children playing in a grassy meadow, rolling and tumbling over a big dog with great freedom. As she approached, the dog broke away from them and came bounding to meet her, crouching and fawning at her feet in welcome. It was her dear Sport, their family dog. She hugged his neck, her head on his silken fur. There, the dog understood every word she spoke. And his hair! He bathed in the river every day and it left a living mark on his coat.

One of the sweetest proofs of our Father's loving care for us is that it seems we will find in heaven the small things that gave us great happiness below.

I am also asked many questions about marriage in heaven. We will know no sorrow there, nor is there any unfulfilled desire that cannot be fully met in heaven. If you did not marry on earth and a godly companion is your deepest need I believe you will be satisfied there. Millions of meaningful relationships will be possible. Definitely there will be no differences in faith, no unequal yoking. I believe there will be personal, intimate relationships in heaven lasting forever, but with no reproduction.

God is love and initiated the idea of mates for Adam and Eve. They "gave in marriage" in order to populate the earth. We are not sure how full the earth would have become had Adam and Eve not sinned and caused death to enter the picture, or how they would have been transported to heaven. We do know, however, that "in the ressurection they neither marry, nor are given in marriage" (Matthew 22:30), there is no death and no need for repopulation to replace lost humanity.

I believe if a woman is pregnant when she dies or when Jesus comes, she will have the first painless childbirth in a place where there is no suffering.

A 22-year-old woman told me she wants a husband but no children. What she wants is heaven!

Some marriages here are made in heaven. I don't think that God will break up a good relationship. If you have a loving relationship with a spouse or sweetheart it will remain in heaven—even be enhanced! There is no reason to believe it will be diminished; indeed, this reunion of sweethearts may be one of heaven's chief joys.

Some companionships have lasted more than half a century and could go on throughout the ages. Why not? The Bible says, "What therefore God has joined together, let no man separate" (Matthew 19:6). I believe some people rush into marriages that were not intended to be in the first place. In heaven God's perfect will shall be done. In heaven it will be as it should have been on earth. I believe God knows a person somewhere made just for you. If you don't find him or her here, perhaps there. If you are happily joined in union with another, your love and oneness will be far sweeter there than it ever was here.

Suppose you have been widowed three times on earth. Which husband or wife will you prefer in heaven?

It is questions like these that make the idea "one per customer" seem like good advice! Perhaps we can think about it this way. In heaven our first love will be Jesus. There is no jealousy or competition there, only unity and harmony. You may well prefer relatives and old friends to new acquaintances, but, in general, everyone will have perfect love for everyone else. Carl and I feel we would be unselfish enough to rejoin our first mates there.

If you still want to pick just one favorite person, King Solomon will be there to help you decide. Or you can ask God Himself, the great Judge of the universe!

On a more serious note, I am often asked about wayward children and heaven. Some parents seem to do everything right and yet their kids go wrong. I think in this situation we must stand on the Word: "For I know whom I have believed, and am persuaded that he is able to keep that which I have committed unto him against that day" (2 Timothy 1:12, KJV).

The prophet Jeremiah said, "Thus says the Lord, 'A voice is heard in Ramah, lamentation and bitter weeping. Rachel is weeping for her children . . . because they are no more. . . . Restrain your voice from weeping, and your eyes from tears; for your work shall be rewarded,' declares the Lord, 'and they shall return from the land of the enemy. And there is hope for your future . . . and your

children shall return to their own territory' " (Jeremiah
31:15–17).

The Bible also tells us, "Train up a child in the way he
should go: and when he is old, he will not depart from it"
(Proverbs 22:6, KJV). Or, as my dad used to tell us, "Do
your best and the Lord will make up the difference."

These Scriptures can help sustain us as we pray for our
children to turn their lives over to the Lord, but how do
we pray when a young person—or adult—has already
died or chooses to end his life by suicide?

When Carl pastored a church in Texas we received a call
to come and support a couple whose seventeen-year-old
son had hanged himself with his belt. I talked with a Christian medical doctor hoping to find help for them.

He said he believed that if a child has been taught of
Jesus, and if someone is currently praying for him, the
child will be given one last chance either to receive or
reject God at the end. This physician believes that a person's mind continues to function for about 56 seconds
after death occurs; a person can do a lot of praying in that
time.

For instance, a man called me to report that he had had
cardiac arrest and had cried out, "Jesus, save me!" He did
not think he would live and wanted to take a leap of faith,
a last plea that God would even consider letting him into
His heaven.

He was given a second chance at life and said he remembered well the last sermon he heard before the heart attack.
The minister's text was: "It is time to seek the Lord" (Ho-
sea 10:12). Recall of the Scripture in that sermon brought
that man to his soul's knees and a rescue prayer at the last
moment.

We can hope that the searching hearts of these young people who have ended their lives reached out to the love of Jesus as well.

We must always cling to God's mercy. There is always hope. Difficult questions like this one about death are where prayer, faith, and trust take hold.

When answers seem hard to find, remember that without Christ something is always wanting. When we are young we have grand enterprises, but no experience. When we are old we have the experience, but then the power and energy to carry out our schemes are gone. In heaven we will have both! "Happy is he that hath the God of Jacob for his help, whose hope is in the Lord his God" (Psalm 146:5, KJV).

We will undoubtedly have many questions about heaven that will have to wait until we arrive there. God doesn't have to explain everything to us here. As we have said earlier, Deity reserves some crown rights. Wait patiently for Him. Time is just nature's way of keeping everything from happening all at once. God's timing and His answers are always on time.

4

Where Is Heaven?

Perhaps my favorite response to the question "Where is heaven?" is a line from an old hymn: "Where Jesus is, 'tis heaven there!" Another song says that "He is as close as the mention of His name."

Heaven is not so far away but that God can hear us when we pray. It is accessible to everyone through prayer. This does not mean, however, that heaven is only an ethereal sort of place, unapproachable in a physical sense. It is a very real place occupied by very real inhabitants. Jesus said He would come back and take us there (John 14:1–4).

Part of the heavenlies must be visible for the Bible tells us that in the last days there will be signs in the heavens (probably the second heaven we identified earlier) and in the earth. Perhaps some of these signs are becoming evident as we learn more about our universe as it relates to heaven.

Astronomers agree, for instance, that there is a huge opening or cavity in the constellation of Orion that is perhaps more than 16,740,000,000,000 miles in diameter. (The diameter of the earth's orbit is about 186,000,000 miles.) Said one telescopic observer from the Mt. Lowe Observatory in New Mexico: "But surpassing the immensity of its size is its exquisite beauty and the luminous colors that are unlike any on earth. The opening and interior are so stupendous that our entire solar system would be lost therein. . . . The depth reveals rivers and masses of shining glass, irregular pillars, columns of stalactites and stalagmites from the mighty floor. The appearance is like that of light shining and glowing behind clear walls of ivory and pearl, studded with millions of diamonds like shining stars."

Is this perhaps a glimpse of a heavenly realm? There must be a reason why all this splendor is lavished on this one spot in the heavens. At any rate, it is no wonder that many scientists claim to feel some almighty presence while scanning this great outburst of grandeur.

Another phenomenal sighting: Dr. Kurt Bauer, an astrophysicist, claims to have viewed photographs taken by a Soviet space probe that seem to resemble heaven. "The pictures are remarkable in their similarity to what people have seen during near-death experiences," he says.

Apparently, in the pictures, darkness gives way to a rainbow-colored tunnel of light. "As [the probe emerges from this tunnel] we are met with an unearthly green and yellow landscape." He further describes a scene that looks like a great walled city emitting an intense golden light.

Bauer claims that hundreds of these pictures were beamed back to earth. Russian officials, apparently, have not confirmed or denied the story. They have said that Bauer worked with Soviet scientists and would have access to any photographs "if they do exist."

Other amazing stories have popped up in the media purporting to relate to heaven and its place in space. The *Houston Chronicle*, for instance, reported in January 1986 that six Soviet cosmonauts claimed to have seen a band of glowing angels. "What we saw," they said, "were seven giant figures in the form of humans, but with wings and mistlike halos, as in the classic depiction of angels." Angels are the messengers of God, traveling from the throne room to the earth to carry out their missions. Could they have been glimpsed en route?

Consider with me this interesting insight on the location of heaven. Isaiah 14:13 tells us that heaven is "above the stars of God" and "in the recesses of the north." Since the stars encircle the earth, "north" could be considered "up" from every part of the earth. Thus, wherever a believer is when he dies, it seems his soul would go "up."

When Paul spoke of being caught up into the third heaven (2 Corinthians 12:2) he not only indicated direction, but he left us to assume that there are first and second heavens as well. These all were completed in the six days of creation (Genesis 2:1), not set in motion as in an evolutionary process, but finished with His mighty power for His wonderful purposes.

The first heaven, as we saw earlier, is the atmosphere around us, the air we breathe, where birds and airplanes fly, where clouds are formed. Matthew 24:30–31 tells us that at the Second Coming of Christ, the sign of the Son of Man will appear in the sky, visible to those on earth, and then Jesus will come "on the clouds of the sky with power and great glory. And He will send forth His angels with a great trumpet and they will gather together His elect from the four winds, from one end of the sky to the other."

The second heaven is the starry space of the firmament above us, where the moon, the stars, and the galaxies revolve. With powerful telescopes, scientists are able to see several quintillion miles into space.

These first two realms are readily visible, though we see only glimpses of the spiritual encounters taking place in them. I mentioned that many Bible scholars feel that this second heaven is where Satan and the angels who rebelled with him were sent when they were expelled from God's presence.

Daniel is possibly a case in point. After fasting and praying he was visited by an angel—perhaps Gabriel—who told of ongoing battles with the princes—satanic angels—of Persia and Greece. These were not taking place within human sight, but seemed nevertheless to relate to places of human habitation.

The third heaven—seen by Paul and John—is God's residence and is far above all the heavens (Ephesians 4:10). This is where God has seated Jesus at His right hand "far above all rule and authority and power and dominion, and every name that is named" (Ephesians 1:21).

Job 22:14 (KJV) says that God walks in the "circuit of heaven." I take this to mean that heaven is a sphere like our earth. Its size is unknown, but *big*, bigger even than the second heaven, which holds a "countless" number of stars (Jeremiah 33:22). If heaven is up in all directions and a sphere, perhaps it encircles our earth in some fashion.

From Revelation 21:16 we learn that the capital city of heaven, the New Jerusalem, is 1,500 miles long, wide, and high. This city would cover about half of the United States— from Maine to Florida and from the Atlantic Ocean to the Colorado River. Though some believe it to be cube-shaped, I like Dr. H. A. Ironside's interpretation that the heavenly Jerusalem is shaped like a pyramid. I would imagine it with the throne at the top. "The glory of God gives it light, and the Lamb is its lamp" (Revelation 21:23, NIV).

Out of the throne and down the middle of the street flows a river of life; on each side of the river stands the tree of life (Revelation 22:1–2).

I've seen a tree more glorious than the white birch in Aspen or Vail, or the jacaranda in Florida. I saw the tree of life during my brief 28-minute death. I want to keep my passport visa in order—and Jesus is the way.

Twelve gates are positioned in the wall around the city, each a single pearl (Revelation 21:21). The gates allow people to enter the city or to go out into what we might consider countryside. The walls around the city consist of twelve layers of gems: sapphires (blue), emeralds (green), sardonyx (pale blue), chrysolite (blue-green), beryl (pale green), topaz (golden yellow), amethyst (purple), and others mentioned in Revelation 21. God promises us that in exchange for sins forgiven and purity here, we will walk on gems. Satan has deceived the world to sell itself short for temporary riches. Jesus wants us to remember where our true riches lie.

The ultimate destiny of earth is being directed from heaven where God is on the throne and Jesus sits at His right hand. Not only are the matters of the universe ordered, history brought to its final stage, but as Mona Johnian puts it in her Bible study of heaven, "God is ordering life in the heavenly realm, a lot of action more significant than we see here on earth." All authority in heaven and on earth is there. It could be that during Christ's Millennial reign on earth we will have ready access to this governing capital.

The Holy Spirit is God's personal proof that heaven is real. He is the signal that Jesus has arrived where He told us He was going (Acts 2:32–33). Just as Jesus has a glorified body (Luke 24:36–43), we, too, will have glorified bodies in heaven. These will be our natural bodies "permanentized." Sometimes we long to exchange our earthly "tent" for that clothing of heaven (2 Corinthians 5:1–3).

Paradise is heaven under God's monarchy and stability. A teacher in Fort Wayne said of heaven, "I've been in a most wonderful place. The next time I go, don't bring me back."

Oden Hetrick, whom I mentioned earlier, described paradise this way: "The sky was gold. So many things there were gold. It seemed to be the central color scheme.

"I went for a swim in the river of life to wash off the last of earth's dust. I swam and splashed without effort. It was more like playing in a park. The river was deep, over my head, but I could breathe underwater. It covered all my scars of sin. The past remorse of my memory was buried there so I could forget it, too, and enjoy heaven. After that washing I felt worthy to be there. . . .

"I knew I was there, deep in solar space, and that earth was a mere shadow of heaven. . . . I knew this was Jesus' home and saw many people who had died. I didn't want to return."

Wherever heaven is, being there is like being in no other place. I am glad, however, that we don't have to wait until we get to heaven to get all of heaven. God has given us a foretaste of our inheritance here. Look at the following letter, for instance.

Two days after reading your book *Angels Watching Over Me* an angel appeared suddenly to me in my bedroom and spoke three words, "Do not fear." Two days later while riding to the hospital coughing up blood hemorrhaged from my lungs, I felt no fear at any time. Four days later when I was released from the hospital there was some old blood in my right lung. Now, two weeks later, there is no evidence of any problem at all.

The book of Isaiah contains this promise: "Before they call I will answer." God had prepared this woman with a little of heaven beforehand to remove her fear.

When we believe in Jesus we, too, have access to heaven on earth through His glorious presence. And someday He will take us to that place far above all we know or see to dwell with Him forevermore.

5

How Do We Feel About Heaven?

I did a telecast recently with C. M. Ward and asked him, "How can a person be sure he or she is going to heaven?"

"Easy," he replied with a smile. "By one word, *looking*. Think about these Scriptures: 'Unto them that look for him shall he appear the second time . . . unto salvation' [Hebrews 9:28, KJV] and 'I will guide thee with mine eye' [Psalm 32:8, KJV]. You can receive intimate eye signals only if you have good eye contact and are paying attention to Him."

I think he's right. Living a few miles away from Carl and me is a man with three stretch limos, a gorgeous, faithful wife, four nice children, and a lover in England. He's not looking for Jesus; he thinks this is heaven. It's my guess that a lot of people who are blasé about heaven are going to be disappointed that they didn't spend more time thinking about it and about what it takes to get there.

My husband pastors a church in Dunedin, Florida. Last summer his associate, Karen Siddle, treated a young family visiting her to a day at Disney World.

Driving home after a fun-packed day, the parents were appreciative, the younger children were happily exhausted and had fallen asleep. But the older boy sat looking out the window.

Karen asked him, "Well, Pete,* what do you think?"
He answered blandly, "Is that all?"

People miss out on a lot of joy in this world by wrong attitudes. Most of us fail to get excited about heaven the way this boy was unimpressed by Disney World. For the individual who is going to heaven, nothing should stir up more enthusiasm. Earthly disappointments are one thing, but heaven cannot be a disappointment. No matter how wonderful we think it will be, it will be more wonderful still. There are many cherished charismatics and pampered Pentecostals who have been singing "Redeemed" for 58 years, but not hearing the words!

I had an experience similar to Karen's but with a different outcome. About three winters ago I brought a young mother of three small boys to Florida for six days. My husband was traveling and her mother-in-law took care of the little fellows.

She had never seen the ocean, never been out of her home state or flown in an airplane! I received more rest, relaxation, and pure joy by showing her things she had never seen than I have for a long time. The remarks of appreciation and expressions of merriment on her face were more rewarding than I can describe.

Think how it must give the Lord pleasure when His children think about heaven with eager anticipation! If we enjoy sharing what we have with others, His delight in sharing the joys of heaven with us must know no bounds.

My Aunt Lillian was the principal of an elementary school in Indiana. Many of her students were poor farm children and offspring of riverboat folks. When one little

---

* Name has been changed.

fellow missed school most of the winter she visited his house to learn they had no heat and had burned most of their furniture in an old coal stove to keep warm. She went home and got help to carry her own couch and chair back to them. When she arrived, the little guy looked at his mother and squealed, "Pretty! Mommy, this is like heaven!"

Can you imagine the utter joy, the wonder and amazement of children arriving in heaven from the underprivileged, starving nations of the world or the countries where people are tortured for their faith?

How different things are in many places in this country! I worked for five years at a jewelry store in New Castle, Indiana, and watched people comb the aisles to find something for a relative that he or she did not already have. One couple told me, "Our grandchildren still have presents in the basement unopened from last year." Some people are so engrossed with the baubles of this world they will miss the glories of the world to come.

We should be excited about heaven! It is the finish line, the end of the race where rewards and trophies will be given. Jesus said, "Be thou faithful unto death, and I will give thee a crown of life" (Revelation 2:10, KJV). In Jesus' parable of the talents, the master said, "Well done, thou good and faithful servant: thou hast been faithful over a few things, I will make thee ruler over many things: enter thou into the joy of thy lord" (Matthew 25:21, KJV).

I like to enhance my perspective of heaven by thinking of it as a place of "no mores." Here are five "no mores" that are at the top of my list.

First, heaven is a place of no more emergencies.

I'm a survivor. I have been through many storms in my

life and I have always found that God is faithful. I'm glad that Jesus is in the prayer-answering business in heaven.

A pastor wrote me: "I was with an elderly lady who was dying. She asked me to pray that God would let her die. I hated to do it, so she prayed: 'I have been faithful, Lord. You have answered a lot of my living prayers; now answer this dying one. Lord, give me a new body. I can't stand this pain. I can't take this sickness any longer.' She quit breathing within five minutes."

Jesus has given us the best of both worlds. In our earthly lives He is working full-time to be our caring Father. He doesn't have a second job or other part-time employment, and we don't have to worry about putting too much work on Him. When we have any problem, any emergency that we can't handle, we can turn to Him.

And in our "heavenly" lives, there will be no emergencies to worry about. No wrong decisions, accidents, carelessness, or evil motives to hurt us.

Second, heaven is a place of no more unforgiveness.

A young couple brought their seven-year-old daughter, Heather, to meet me and sent her out to play while they told me an amazing story.

The little girl had dived into the deep end of their backyard swimming pool, and they found her drowned, floating face down. The paramedics arrived in three or four minutes. In the emergency room of the hospital after a miraculous recovery from death, Heather gave her mother a curious message. She looked at her mother and said, "Grandma says she forgives you." Heather had never seen even a photograph of her grandmother, but was able to describe her—her size, her hair, the mole near her left ear.

Heather's mother told me she was taken aback at this

message. She had become pregnant with Heather out of wedlock and when her parents learned of it, they dismissed her from their home and told her never to return. A year later, after she had married and the little girl had been born, she tried to locate her parents only to learn they had moved. She destroyed all photos of her parents and hate festered in her heart for years.

Then she became born again and wanted to let her parents know she forgave them for their harsh reaction; Jesus had forgiven her fornication and she hoped they would, too. She and her husband began to pray for her parents' salvation.

Finally, soon after the drowning incident, they were able to locate her father and learned that her mother had died four weeks previously.

This young woman, Heather's mother, was able to put her heart at rest because of the unusual message her daughter brought back from heaven.

Forgiveness is the order of the day in heaven. Perhaps we will understand as never before the enormous gift of forgiveness that God has given us through His Son, Jesus Christ, and our own grievances will seem petty in the light of that love.

Third, heaven is a place of no more pollution.

This doesn't just include the pollution of our oceans and rivers and air. It includes the pollution in our nations of drugs, alcohol, greed, perversion.

I read an article this year about a teenager in Finland who is suing his parents for a million dollars because he says they brought him into this world without his consent to a life he feels is painful and fraught with hardship. The attorney, Erkki Kantola, says, "He may just have a case."

Other stories closer to home tell of hate and murder in families and neighborhoods.

Thank God there will be no sexual perversion, no homosexuals or lesbians (Romans 1:26–29; 1 Corinthians 6:9–10). Jesus can break the chains of deception and release the captives from that prison. "Such were some of you: but ye are washed . . . sanctified . . . justified in the name of the Lord Jesus, and by the Spirit of our God" (1 Corinthians 6:11, KJV).

His blood can cleanse from all sin, but we must want the change. We must quit our sin. Then we can enjoy the purity of heaven, the unpolluted countryside, thoughts, and actions awaiting us there.

Fourth, heaven is a place of no more unsung heroes.

Heaven will reveal a different perspective on accomplishments. I am anxiously awaiting awards night up there. We will have eternity to stage many awards sessions for the faithful, the anonymous, the people whose integrity has been consistent—the *always* people.

Here we tend to applaud the gifted; magazines parade the pretty; men slobber over the shapely; but there everyone gets his just and earned rewards.

I love snow at Christmas, but I lived in the Dakotas where we had snow on the ground one year for eight months. We had two seasons, July and winter.

Those sturdy Dakotans are real people, working to grow grain for us, loving their families where there are few trees and the wind blows freely and the wind chill factor zooms down to 125 degrees below zero. One year we had below zero temperatures for 64 days. In heaven the Dakotans will probably live in the southern clime on the sunny side!

"For God is not unrighteous to forget your work and

labour of love, which ye have shown toward his name, in that ye have ministered to the saints, and do minister" (Hebrews 6:10, KJV).

First Corinthians speaks of the ministry of helps. What a great career, though it is not heralded much in this life! Counseling, exhorting (which means encouraging), serving, teaching, giving, showing mercy. In heaven, the people who have been about these occupations will be properly honored and rewarded.

My friend Sara Douglas was a giver. I'm sure she will administer in the "Giving Department" up there. She was always giving fruit, flowers, books, clothes, time on the phone, and useful reading materials here. I have no doubt that Esther Zink and Paul and Mona Johnian will be executives in heaven's great book and tape library. They have shared their materials unselfishly and generously.

I know two ladies who don't want to reveal their names, but who have prayed for a Dakota boy for 22 years. He is now a gifted neurosurgeon. When they all get to heaven, those two will share in his rewards.

Fifth, heaven is a place of no more stressful, unhappy, or unfulfilling work.

God created work and it is good. When Adam and Eve sinned in the Garden, however, work turned into grueling labor.

It is true that many people have jobs they enjoy. This is something of a mirror image of the way work was meant to be. These people marvel that they receive payment for jobs they would do without any reimbursement.

For the most part, however, this is not the case. Many women, for instance, have been deserted by their husbands and left alone to support their children. Many men find it hard to meet bills and payments on meager salaries.

In heaven they can rest from their labors. I believe there will be work there, but it will be the kind of labor that invigorates us, that thrills us with its fulfillment. It will be the thing we love doing most, and we will do it for the honor of our Lord Jesus.

There are plenty other "no mores" in heaven: No more death, sorrow, or sickness. (I met a little old lady in the hospital. Her name was Ida Ill and she said, "With a name like that, I've been sick all my life!" Then I saw an epitaph on a tombstone in Milwaukee that said, "I told you I was sick!")

No more racing the clock. We will have all eternity to accomplish our goals, our deepest desires. We will get everything done.

No more separation from the Prince of Peace. There will be political harmony, for the government will be upon His shoulders. No war, no weapons, no fear of attack from another nation.

And there are still more! Look at this list:

no more hurricanes	no more stress	no more fear
no more separation	no more weeds	no more sin
no more storms	no more thorns	no more wor
no more limitations	no more night	no more lock
no more cancer	no more want	no more pai
no more tears	no more clocks	no more med
no more judgment	no more decay	no more gui
no more alcohol abuse	no more bad habits	no more dru

---

* Worry is today's mice nibbling on tomorrow's cheese.

A mother wrote me from Washington state that in a dream she saw her son for whom she was grieving. He told her, "Don't wish me back. You forget I was born blind. I am *seeing* the wonders of glory here." She said her grieving ended.

I have heard that Billy Graham had a vision of his grandfather who had lost a leg and an eye in the Civil War. He was complete, walking and seeing.

And I spoke with a handicapped man who has been frail since birth. He said during prayer one morning he was given a vision of sporting events in heaven. It was thrilling to see because an athlete's body will not be hindered there and can reach its greatest potential with God's power and strength.

Walking along at those heavenly Olympics, he noticed a young man, his marvelous back muscles flexing as he threw the shot put. When the athlete turned, the man saw it was *his* face! He is looking forward to heaven with an eager perspective because he believes he will be there what he always wanted to be here.

All puzzles complete . . . all missing parts restored better than new. We shall stand complete in Him!

Does this undergird your perspective about heaven? It does mine! And it tells me something else. While people can change our perspectives about heaven, heaven changes our perspectives about people.

When my life came to a screeching halt in that hospital room, I recalled the saying, "You can't take it with you." I had never been sick. Now I lay dying and realized that I had never liked people, but that people—those we had helped find salvation—were all we could take with us to eternity. When God gave me a second chance to live, I returned with a new perspective, the desire to invest in people. "People" is the only commodity that transfers from this life to the next.

From its creation, heaven has been a marvelous, complete place, always inhabited with angels and palatial splendor. But from the beginning God wanted something more. He wanted people to be there, too.

People are important to Him. He does not wish that any should perish (2 Peter 3:9). For God the Father created people, Jesus died for people, and the Holy Spirit indwells people.

We all know those who have invested in people. I once got a letter written in a feeble hand. The old man asked, "Do you know of any pill to cure loneliness?" For some time my Aunt Gwen corresponded with him. He loved to get something in his mailbox.

The same day I got his letter, I got a letter from Sue Sharp in Kentucky. She said she felt a prompting in her heart to drive across town and check on an elderly friend. She started to shrug it off because it meant battling afternoon rush hour traffic, but her heart would not let her ignore it. She arrived to find her friend too incapacitated to reach for the phone and summon help.

As we invest in people we realize that we are many times on the receiving end of others' investments. One day, while carrying two cartons of blooming plants down the path shortcutting home, I met Carolyn.

"Honey," she said, "tell me that you didn't *buy* those." She took me to her house. "My yard is overgrown with anything that grows in Florida." Now my yard looks like Eden. She has given me some of everything she has.

Carolyn has a wonderful perspective on helping others.

Early one morning I decided to walk my three miles before it got too hot. There was Carolyn down on the beach picking up cans and trash. I asked her if she was the beach angel.

"No," she said, "I'm the original bag lady. I come every morning and evening and tidy up the beach. While I'm here I get to enjoy the sunrise and sunset. I don't guess I've missed a single one in twenty-six years."

This woman lives alone but isn't lonely. She has a merry heart, and in giving of herself receives enjoyment from the beauty of the world around her.

Little things can mean a lot when we invest in others. Last February I sent a valentine to the most despised, hateful, selfish woman in the state of Illinois. I met her some time ago and her miserable reputation of greed had followed her for many years.

I was amazed to receive a note from her. She wrote, "This is the first valentine I have gotten since I was a girl thirteen years old." It broke her heart. Her neighbors tell me she has made a drastic change since then.

Our perspectives on heaven and the people we help find it are important to the way we live our lives now. We can keep that perspective aligned by praising Jesus for the joy of eternity with Him, and by sharing that good news with others.

Few things can be more exciting!

6

Hell, the Involuntary Alternative

Satan doesn't mind if you talk about him or his domain. He doesn't care if you meanmouth him, so long as you don't talk to God and about Jesus. I refuse to give free advertisement on a page in this book, but I do not think one can adequately write about heaven without mentioning the involuntary alternative, hell, which is also a permanent dwelling place.

One man wrote me: "My veins collapsed for the third time after a heart attack. Light and dark waged a war. Suddenly all was black as night in the Carlsbad Caverns in New Mexico when tourists are taken far beneath the earth's surface and the lights are cut off momentarily. My spirit left my body like pulling the stopper out of a thermos bottle. Faster and faster it traveled at an approximate 45 degree angle. I saw horrors, undescribable pitch blackness. I thought, *This must be hell*. . . ."

The Scriptures are plain: "Do not be deceived, God is not mocked; for whatever a man sows, this he will also reap" (Galatians 6:7). "All have sinned and fall short of the glory of God" (Romans 3:23). We are lost unless we cling to the saving grace of Jesus. As the hymn says,

> My hope is built on nothing less
> Than Jesus' blood and righteousness. . . .

His oath, His covenant, His blood
Support me in the whelming flood.

When I was a child Mother used to tell us, If you never play with matches you'll never burn the house down. It followed: If you don't try smoking, you'll never have to kick the habit; if you never taste alcohol, you'll never become a drunkard. (It's true. I never saw anyone become a drunkard all at once.)

We used to play a game called "First he took a nibble, then he took a bite." Sin is like that. It can seem so innocent or insignificant at first, but unchecked or unrepented of can lead to the loss of your soul. Satan does not announce his motive to damn our souls. He tries to deceive us into sinning and to bluff us into thinking there's no way out. Beware: There is no right way to do wrong.

In some parts of India they worship snakes. Many people refuse to kill them. I saw a newspaper article describing how one came into a home and coiled around the neck of a six-month-old baby. The child was found dead. Serpents of sin—drunkenness, pride, adultery—are slipping into our homes unawares whenever we open the doors to them even a crack.

Some take God's mercy to mean that He will never send a soul to hell. They are not considering that God is a righteous Judge. Suppose the governor of a state could not bear to see anyone punished for breaking the law and pardoned everyone the courts had ever convicted. He would not be governor for long. The state would be unsafe.

God has certain laws, too. He has told us clearly that we must repent of our sins (Acts 17:30) and believe in the

Lord Jesus Christ (Romans 10:9) in order to be saved. Scripture says that "whoever believes in Him will not be disappointed" (Romans 10:11). Those who don't will be.

I spent some time with Dr. Maurice Rawlings, a heart specialist and author of *Beyond Death's Door*. He told me that of the patients whose deaths he witnessed, eighty percent had a horrible experience and only twenty percent had a peaceful experience. The Bible says that strait is the gate, narrow the way that leads to life, and few there be that find it.

He also said that while people described hellish experiences immediately upon returning to life, they later seemed to forget them or put them out of their minds. Dr. Rawlings said, "The evil god of this world, Satan, has blinded their eyes so they cannot remember and warn others."

But some have had their lives changed by the experience and have warned us. Dr. George Ritchie has written of the desolation he felt at being asked: "What did you do with your life?" The deeds he had thought to be so important seemed minuscule under the scrutiny of that question.

He saw miserable people writhing in agony trying to make up to their living loved ones for hurts they had caused, particularly from suicide. He saw people chained to the consequences of their behaviors, for all eternity powerless to satisfy themselves. He saw people fighting, gouging each other, but never dying, howling with despair.

Then in the distance he saw a light—Jesus, the light of the world. He returned to life and had a second chance to tell others about Jesus.

Here are some last words of famous people.

Voltaire, an atheist, spent his last few months in such remorse and fear of hell that his nurse said she would never again attend a dying atheist.

Edward Gibbon, philosopher, author of *The Decline and Fall of the Roman Empire* and an infidel, died with these words: "All is now lost, finally irrecoverably lost. All is dark and doubtful."

Atheist Thomas Hobbes died in Devonshire, England, saying: "I am about to take a leap in the dark, and I shall be glad to find a hole [into which] to creep out of the world's misery."

Cardinal Beaufort Winchester, half-brother to King Henry IV, said these last words: "And must I then die? Will not my riches save me? I could purchase the kingdom if that would prolong my life. Alas, there is no bribing death!"

Sir Francis Newport was dying as a young man. "Wretch that I am," he said, "what will become of me?" An infidel companion tried to dispel his fears but he replied, "There is a God, I know. I am equally sure there is a hell. All sins are brought to my remembrance. I was religiously educated so my torment is greater than if I had not known. Oh, the insufferable pangs of hell!"

A minister told the story of being overtaken by a thunderstorm in his travels and seeking refuge in a tavern. There he could not help overhearing a man using profanity, boasting of his atheism, and blaspheming the name of God.

Finally the man stated, "There is no God, and to prove it . . . I will go out and dare Him to strike me with His lightning."

Once out in the storm he shook his fist toward heaven

in defiance. Then he came in and said, "You can see for yourselves that there is no God. If there were, He would have killed me while daring Him to do so."

Then he took a chair and was quiet for some time. When he spoke again it was apparent his attitude had taken a change. "There is a God," he said, "and He is going to teach me that he can take my life with a smaller instrument than a shaft of lightning. Soon after I came in here a little insect lit upon my hand and stung it. It commenced to pain me and soon affected my arm and is fast doing its fatal work. I shall soon be a dead man, and my soul will be in hell. Yes, there is a God."

The minister reported that the man died in awful agony of body and mind. As the Scripture says, "Surely the fool hath said in his heart, 'There is no God.' "

Ethan Allen, a noted infidel, wrote a book against the divinity of the Lord. His wife, a devoted Christian, died leaving a young daughter who became the idol of her father. Now the daughter was dying of tuberculosis. He begged her not to die, but she replied, "Doctor says I will die today. . . . Mother told me about the Savior who died for us all and He sits enthroned in glory. . . . Shall I accept Him as she, or reject Him as you have taught me?"

Speaking through tears, Allen replied, "My child, cling to your mother's Savior. She was right. I'll try to follow you to that blessed abode."

We, too, must seek Him while He may be found. God had one Son. He lived a sinless life, died at Calvary, and conquered death by rising from the grave. The Holy Spirit is our Comforter, the One alongside us to help us choose to follow Jesus.

Once flying from Tampa I fell asleep and woke to hear

the attendant announce: "After a brief stop in Dallas, this plane will continue to Phoenix. Unless you want to continue with this flight you must deplane."

Because of our sins, we are headed like passengers on a plane for one destination, hell. But we can choose to "deplane" and repent of the lives we are living and take a flight for another destination. Not making the change is the same as choosing to remain off-course. If you're headed in the wrong direction, repent and transfer before it's too late.

Our friend Sara Douglas shared a dream with me recently from years before that had changed her life. She dreamed she went to a reception hall. Most of her friends were there, but she had a dreadful feeling she should not be. They were glad she was with them, but there was no gladness in her heart. When she awakened, she began searching for the Way, and found it.

On earth the law of gravity pulls everything down. In heaven everything is up, up toward the throne of God, bounding upward with spiritual gravitation. Just as there are two poles to a magnet, positive and negative, so all souls will be drawn toward one of two places. God's throne is the center of His everlasting Kingdom of light and toward it all gracious spirits who are blood-washed are drawn from the time they accept Jesus.

In heaven there is all life and no death. In hell there is all death and no life. Here on earth there is both living and dying, which is between the two. If we are dead to sin here, we have truly begun to live.

7

The Journey Starts Here

I love to think of this saying, "The journey to the house of a friend is never long," in relation to Jesus. "What a Friend we have in Jesus," the hymn proclaims. We're on our way on the journey to heaven and can rejoice even if the going gets bumpy now and then. The goal makes the journey worthwhile.

My new word processor, for example, has made the journey through this book bumpy, but I'm not distracted because I have a goal.

One morning I had a chapter completed and ready to print out. The phone rang and I got distracted from the main road onto a short side trip. Consequently, I pushed the wrong button and wiped out the chapter. Later that day a man came to the door and I locked myself out of my writing studio. I lost two hours of work, $30 for a locksmith, and, rushing upstairs to get the money, I fell, turned my ankle, bruised my elbow, and howled pitifully.

But I got up and kept going because I had a goal that meant more to me than any inconvenience along the way.

Last year I traveled 192,000 miles on a number of trips. After each one several people would ask the same question: "How was your trip?" The answer was usually the same: I was glad to be home, particularly from the rough rides.

Our journey to heaven is like these examples. Heaven is our ultimate goal, our long-awaited home, and we can anticipate our arrival on each day of our journey through this life. It doesn't matter where you come from, but it does matter where you are going and how you get there. God only cares that you walk with Him.

Here are six principles we can follow to enhance the journey, to be assured that we walk with Him.

First, we must "walk our talk."

For Christmas Carl and I both got navy-and-orange sweatshirts from Wheaton College where our daughter April is captain of the women's basketball team. All over the back of the sweatshirts are footprints and the slogan, "Walk your talk: Job 22:22." She had been appointed designer of the warm-up sweats and wanted to convey this idea from Scripture: Obey the rules, keep them in your heart, and the Lord will be your defense. In other words, don't just talk about basketball, play the game. Talk is cheap. It's what you do, the follow-through, that counts.

On our journey to heaven we must walk our talk as well. Satan is going to do all he can to trip us up, so it is vital to keep our hearts on Jesus and our minds on the goal, heaven.

Last year I spoke at a lovely church in Alberta, Canada, pastored by Wally Reihl. It was near Eastertime and when I described my death experience we had no idea how close Wally was to the end of his journey.

I received a letter from his wife, Erica, recently and she told me how Wally had preached two sermons, his last two it turned out, on heaven. Then he had suffered a heart attack and died shortly after.

Erica said she wore white to the funeral instead of black. "It is not time to focus on lonely me," she wrote, "but to point people to Jesus, to heaven, the place where Wally waits."

Wally walked his talk. He was a "little Christ," naturally and sincerely, and made the journey pleasant for his wife, his children, and his church. And in his death, Erica showed another example of walking with God on the journey.

Second, we should love life along the journey.

Sometimes we need to slow down and sip, not gulp as we go along the way. I get aggravated when people damn this world. The Bible says that God declared His creation good. The apostle Paul wrote that God's "eternal power and divine nature . . . [are] understood through what has been made" (Romans 1:20).

I have started riding my bike or walking to the post office each morning, even if it rains and I have to listen to the pleasant patter on the umbrella. That way I can hear the birds, see the blooming flowers, smile at people, and have them greet me with their kind voices.

Bill Van Garven lived across the street from us in North Dakota. He works at the post office—hard and fast all day. But when he can he retreats to the woods to help him slow his pace and regain a love for life. He sent me this:

> It's miraculous how the depth and serenity of a hunt for elusive whitetails along a wooded creek, or a patient walk through the soft, pleasant atmosphere of nature, drains all the tension and confusing thoughts

from a person's mind. All the elements of nature work like a prescribed medicine to lift your spirits and cleanse your frustrated soul. After only a few deep breaths and several minutes among the oaks and willows, you're freed of society's grasping control.

You soon forget about money pressures, social problems, the unmowed lawn, or the broken window in the garage. Gradually a smile spreads across your face as you begin to feel positive about life, about yourself. You feel sympathy toward those who haven't the desire or time to experience this simple gift. And when you leave the life-giving woodlands and return to the concrete world, you can hold your head high and step lively.

If we take the time to love life we will find the Creator a ready Companion on our walks toward heaven.

Third, we should release our burdens to Jesus along the way. Jesus said, "Come to Me and I will give you rest for the journey." You will find that the cares don't disappear, but the burden of the cares and work will.

I have found that burdened spirits often lead to physical problems, notably, for some reason, with digestion. I don't think our systems can work properly if we try to carry a load too heavy for them. We need to learn to rest in our Father's ability to take our abilities and bring us security. He will enable us to prevail in every situation. After His rest, we can perform our responsibilities and continue the journey toward the goal.

Not all burdens have to be big, important ones in order to weigh us down. Small frustrations affect us, too. If you don't think little things mean a lot, trying pulling your thumb out of a noose of Scotch tape, or tripping on a shoestring while you're jogging! It's not usually the big mountains in our paths that make life hard, it's the small pebbles in our shoes.

We know there are rewards in heaven in exchange for our burdens, but there are often rewards on the journey, too.

My first baby had colic. The only reason I didn't lose my mind or sell her for 59¢ plus tax was the fact that Dr. Ben Harrison assured me it would only last three to six months. I'm glad I persevered! She has brought me 35 years of pride and joy.

History hurrahs David for throwing a stone at Goliath. It was a risk, but someone had to do it and it seems that no one else was even considering it. David, appalled that anyone should so reproach Israel, gambled, put his faith in God, and won. It was a simple battle, just God and a rock.

His valor was not without rewards, pleasures for the journey. First Samuel 17:25 tells us that whoever killed the giant would be enriched by the king with great wealth, receive the king's daughter as a bride, and never have to pay taxes the rest of his life. (I'd almost join the army for that last benefit. Have you paid Florida taxes lately?)

It will help us on the journey to remember that even Jesus "for the joy set before Him endured the cross, despising the shame" (Hebrews 12:2). He remained faithful during His walk through the earth because He knew heaven was waiting for Him at the end of His journey here.

Scripture says: "Let us hold fast the confession of our hope without wavering, for He who promised is faithful. . . . Do not throw away your confidence, which has a great reward. For you have need of endurance, so that when you have done the will of God, you may receive what was promised. For yet in a very little while, He who is coming will come, and will not delay" (Hebrews 10:23, 35–37).

Fourth, as we move forward on the journey we should take someone with us.

Peggy Karey wrote an article in which she told this story. She was hurrying through a railway station and barely paused to toss a coin into the hat of a crippled man who was selling pencils. Then she stopped, went back, and asked for her pencil. "He wasn't a beggar," she wrote. "He was a businessman."

Some months later she bought a book at a newsstand in the same station. "I've been looking for you," the owner said to her. She recognized him as the man who had been selling pencils. "You were the first person who ever treated me like a businessman, and now you can see what your encouragement meant to me. I am a businessman."

The way we treat each other is very important. In fact, future life in heaven grows out of our choices in this life. We are the bundle of relationships we develop. Hence, this present life is really the only place where we can determine what type of life we will enjoy in the next real world.

Carl, from his theological/pastoral perspective, puts it this way:

The end of the age as described in the Word of God is to be marked by judgment, Tribulation, and destruction, and finally the earth itself being renovated by fire. The apocalyptic vision itself serves as a catalyst for every Christian: "The earth passeth away and the fashion thereof, but he that doeth the will of God abideth forever." In the light of this revelation we see the sinners around us—the unsaved of the world— unwarned, unaware that time is merging for them into a crisis eternity. Every footstep in time has an echo in eternity, and just as those in Kora's rebellion found eternity beneath their feet (an earthquake swallowed them), and David, too, recognized that he was but a step from death, so time's form is "now" but time's substance is eternal.

The choice is "now" but the results of choice are eternal.

The opportunity for reaching souls is "now." The results of our efforts or our failure will be eternal.

Evangelist Lowell Lundstrom, president of Trinity College, is one of the few ministers I know who never closes a service without inviting people to receive Jesus and salvation.

His journey began in Peever, South Dakota, population 104. There was a gas station, a feed store, and a tavern. Lowell spent every Saturday evening until dark peeping into the doorway of that bar watching a man play a guitar. By watching the fingering closely, he was able to learn to play as well. Later he was born again and chose to play his guitar to worship the Lord and lead others to Him.

My dad's journey required some hard choices, too. During the Depression he had to quit college. Jobs could not be found. For a while we lived with my grandparents. Then when my baby brother, Don, was born, we moved into an old run-down country house that we could fix up for free rent. One time all we had to eat for two days was one boiled potato.

One morning Mother grew worried when she saw Dad take his last shotgun shell and head for the woods. When she heard the shot she was terrified that he might have taken his life. Five minutes later she learned that as he contemplated ending his failure as a provider, the skinniest rabbit you ever saw ran across his path. We had boiled rabbit for three days.

Eventually my father pioneered nine small churches that he built with his own hands.

When I lay in a coma, Art Lindsey from Toad Hop, Indiana, population 48, came and read the Word to me. Since then he has become a prison chaplain and has won many to the Lord.

Small miracles grow into larger ones. God uses ordinary people when He gets ready to do something extraordinary. We shouldn't frown on the journey. Smith Wigglesworth said, "We must look at earth's problems from heaven's standpoint."

We can do little things for each other to encourage ourselves in our walk with God. Most of my driving is along Highway 19. It reminds me of the battle of Armageddon; sometimes there are four wrecks in a mile. It's frightening—and maddening, but once in a while someone will have compassion on you and let you in line. Little things like that, little sacrifices can help us be grateful for others and reach out in return.

One July I was invited to speak in Arizona for six days, and wondered at first why they hadn't invited me to come in February instead! The temperature ranged from 105 to

115 degrees. But the journey! The people I stayed with were a tonic, so pleasant. And let me tell you about my sneakers.

For the trip to Arizona I packed three pairs of high heels and washed my old "holes-in-the-toes" Reeboks to take along, too. (I had rescued them from the garbage once when April threw them away.) Since spinal surgery I must walk every day. I put the shoes on the porch to dry and figured I wouldn't forget them since I practically had to stumble over them coming out of the door.

Well, hurrying to the airport I missed them. In Arizona I told my hostess, Barbara Nelson, that I needed to buy a pair of walking shoes. I didn't mention that I didn't have the money for them, but hoped that somewhere along the line from a love offering I would.

That same morning in the prayer breakfast I saw a woman hand Barbara a pair of Reebok walking shoes exactly like my old worn ones at home—but these were brand-new.

The women came over to me and I joked, "Are those in case you run out of gas and have to walk home?"

"No," the woman said. "These are for you. They arrived this morning and I wondered if you had any use for them."

It so happened that the woman's brother was stationed in Korea near the Reebok factory. She had asked him to send her a pair, size 9. He had mailed her a size 8—my size—by mistake.

Along the journey, God planned a beautiful pair of shoes in my size to arrive from Korea just when I would be in Arizona and need them. They had arrived three weeks late, but on time for me! God cares about our backs and our feet as we walk the journey from here to there.

Fifth, we should make full use of our enthusiasm and humor.

These qualities are all around us, and how they liven up the journey! I spoke at Zion Bible College in Barrington, Rhode Island, for graduation weekend. The topic of our dinner conversation turned toward heaven and led to this exchange.

Jack Mitchell's wife, Bert, asked him, "Jack, if I die before Jesus comes, will you remarry?"

With mischief in his smile, he responded, "Sure. You know I don't like to go to funerals by myself."

We hooted with laughter.

My husband, Carl, is 66. He is full of fun and enthusiasm. He wrote a book called *If You're Over the Hill, You Oughta Be Goin' Faster*. He wakes up early each morning looking for a fresh new challenge, another mountain to climb while pastoring his church and waiting for the Rapture.

I remember from my childhood many times, early morning, my grandpa Dad Perky would stand by the east window and whisper, "Maybe today!" His enthusiasm for heaven gave him enthusiasm for life.

I think my dad, who is full of the joy of life, will go out with gusto. He lives on my brother Jim's ranch. His favorite cow, Tinker Bell, had been missing for four days. She is somewhere between 16 and 24 years old and caring for her is part of my father's loving routine.

Down a gravel road from him live some people who have gained a questionable reputation. When anything is missing, the sheriff usually finds it there.

Neighborhood ranchers were offering help by planning

reports and strategies. My dad simply donned his purple and orange cap, walked down the rocky road to the rustlers' thicket, opened the gate, and called, "Come on, Tinker Bell. Let's go home." She knew his voice. She and her calf followed him the whole way. It must have been some picture!

Living each day with enthusiasm is like being a child with a new toy.

Sixth, we should keep our eyes on Jesus for every step of the journey.

David Mains tells the story about walking through a smelly garbage section of Montreal when, suddenly, he noticed a beautiful fragrance. Looking to the side he saw several girls from the perfume factory on a lunch break. They were permeated with the fragrance because of their constant exposure to it.

I believe we can be saturated with the light of Jesus, till people will know where we have been, and where we are going.

We can be like the old song:

> Shut in with God in a secret place,
> There in the Spirit beholding His face,
> Gaining new power to run in life's race.
> I long to be shut in with God.

Shut in with Him, but not shutting people out in their need. Not isolated from reality, but insulated by a taste of the help Jesus is ready to give us, often through angels, His divinely appointed helpers. Look at these letters I have received about God helping people along the journey:

Grandma took me and my three-year-old sister to McDonald's tonight. We were ten cents short of what we needed at the cash register. I bowed my head and prayed. Right there a man gave me a quarter, then he was gone, we couldn't find him. It might have been an angel, because the devil wouldn't bless God's children, would he?

Love, Enosh, Tracie, and Grandma Fee

This one came from an eleven-year-old in Southboro, Massachusetts:

My mother, sister, and I went swimming. I got away from them in an undertow. I could not scream for help because my face was pounding the ocean floor and my mouth was hurt and full of sand. I felt hands under my armpits pull me out and take me to my mother and sister on the shore. He was gone. There was no one else on the beach before or after but us three. I believe the Word, "It rains on the just and the unjust alike." I didn't know Jesus then. He watches over us even before we know Him. He saved my life, then my soul.

Love, Helen

This letter came from a professional fisherman in Alaska, Clarence Straits, who wrote me about an experience he had had while fishing rough waters on a hazardous day:

I was running the hydraulic winch that turns to pick up about 5,000 pounds of fish. I hooked the bag, had lifted it to the top of the rail, when we hit a wave and lost all but one scrap on the winch. There was no

way I could have held that much fish there. It should
have hurled me around the winch and through the
rigging. Suddenly everything slowed down; a wave
came and set the bag of fish back for me. There must
have been an angel assisting.

I grew up near the coalmining town of Rockville, Indiana, where my dad pastored. I don't know how those
miners could go underground before daylight and come
home after dark. And there were so many cave-ins. Many
times my dad would go to the shaft and elevator door and
stand in the rain and cold waiting for news after a shale
slide, hoping for reports of "alive."

What kept them going on such a hard journey? They
looked forward to attending an old-fashioned, Jesus-
loving church where they found His joy to hold them from
Sunday to Sunday through the week, and the hope of
heaven up ahead. Love kept them down there, making a
living for children and wives. One brawny picker told me,
"The soul afraid of dying never frees up and learns to
live." If we have our eyes on Jesus we can't see fear at the
same time.

Jesus said to occupy until He comes. Enjoy the journey!
We shouldn't just dream of heaven; we should do something on the journey until then. I believe He wants us to
have a good life here. And we can start by teaching our
next generation, if Jesus tarries, the old path of "seeking
Him early." Seek Him early in a situation before it gets out
of hand. Seek Him early each morning before we get side-
tracked. Seek Him early in life while we are young, before
the cares of life or deceitfulness of riches choke us.

Abraham spent his entire life en route to the place where

the builder and maker is God. His faith was attached to the capital city of heaven. Set your affections long-range. Will the things worrying you now really trouble you six months from now?

We have all of eternity to celebrate the victories, but only a few hours before sunset to win them. And in the ages to come He will show us "the exceeding riches of his grace in his kindness toward us" (Ephesians 2:7, KJV).

Dawn Wagler, an artist/writer friend of mine, is writing a Mother's Day article on the sounds and smells of home. Do you remember the sounds from the kitchen of your mother scraping the skillet, pouring the gravy? It was, she reminds us, the last thing before dinner was ready, your signal that it was time to come. And when you arrived, the welcome aroma made you feel happy and fulfilled.

Now we can imagine that in heaven the Marriage Supper of the Lamb is being prepared. We are almost within sight of home, and soon we will get the call that all is ready.

"Come and sup with Me," He will say. And we will have arrived. The journey will be over.

8

Rehearsal for Heaven

When Carl and I were engaged to be married, he would sometimes call and ask to come over for dinner. I'm not sure if he was lonely for a family, hungry for a home-cooked meal, or honestly checking me out to see if I could cook.

All afternoon before the 5:00 arrival of Carl and his little daughter, Connie, I would clean house, groom my children, perfume my hair, burn incense in the dining room to camouflage the scorch smells, put a linen tablecloth on the table, fold napkins with the corners mitered to match those of any expensively wrapped Christmas present, light pale pink candles, and wait for their arrival.

He did not arrive as an afterthought, bring his leftover charm, leftover energy, leftover time to me. He did not bark a menu of what he demanded to eat. He came looking and acting sharp, his best. He appreciated what I had chosen to prepare and serve.

Just as most married couples start out with true appreciation for one another, so we give our best to Jesus when we first come to know Him. And just as couples often hit an eight-year plateau, so we tend to level off in our relationship with Jesus. Jesus chastises a group of believers in Revelation by saying, "I have this against you, that you have left your first love" (2:4).

Remember how excited you were when you first found

Jesus, His love and forgiveness, His healing? How you started worshiping with other believers and became part of a church? This is what Revelation means about losing our first love. It's called backsliding. The heart of the Prodigal Son had traveled to that faraway country, away from his family and his God, long before his feet went there.

As I was growing up, Wednesday night was Bible study and testimony night in our church. My dad would walk down the aisle and ask, "Does anyone have a testimony, a witness for the Lord tonight? Maybe you've had an unusual experience or a prayer answered that you want to share to encourage others to believe to receive an answer to theirs."

One particular night my mother brought the house down with her testimony. She had had a dream.

"I have become entangled with fears, worry, concern about finances, children's communicable diseases, and the cares of life in general," she told us, "until I have not been praying or reading my Bible the way I used to when I was first saved.

"I dreamed last night that Jesus came. I heard the trumpet blow announcing the Rapture. I was in the chicken yard near our orchard feeding cracked corn to our chickens. I didn't go up, so I started leaping and jumping and bouncing upward hoping to take off with the people I had seen rise immediately.

"I looked up and my children and husband had a great headstart on me. I was both heartbroken and horror-struck, but I finally got off the ground. I soared above the apple orchard. I looked down when suddenly I backslid and fell downward. Lying on my back I heard the squawking of the hens and roosters crowing mockingly. I had fallen on my back and was in the chicken lot.

"When I awoke," she concluded, "I determined to revive my first love for Jesus and begin Rapture practice!"

When she told this I was only about seven years old, but I have never forgotten that story. God usually uses humor to minister truths ever so solemn to me.

I had not heard that expression *Rapture practice* for 51 years until I saw it recently in a Christian newsletter I received. It showed a picture of a Victorian house with the sign out front reading *Estate Sale*. Suddenly the owners were dead and everything else was left behind.

We cannot practice for the Rapture—that great gathering and transporting of believers to heaven (see 1 Thessalonians 4:16–18)—by storing up treasures. One day all our keepsakes, all the things we put into closets, into vaults, and on our curio shelves, will be left behind. Only the treasures of love, the hours spent in prayer and daily devotions, the wisdom we store from the Bible will go with us beyond this life.

We still have time to rehearse for the future, to clean out our closets, to hang only loosely onto our possessions and valuables, and concentrate on durable riches, lasting treasures. It's almost enough to make you want to go out to the backyard and practice jumping up and down!

The Scriptures tell us to lay aside every weight that would hold us back, and to get rid of everything that would sidetrack us (Hebrews 12:1–2). The Phillips translation of these verses says we should get rid of the sins that "dog our feet." An apt description!

The King James Version calls them things that "so easily beset us." That could also mean the things that so easily *upset* us, like people not returning books we lent them, a cranky salesperson, or following someone who lets a door slam in our faces. Our attitudes are vitally important. How many opportunities we have to add new treasures to our heavenly store!

If Jesus were coming tomorrow morning, would you make any major changes in the way you live today? Are you ready?

Just after hurricane Elena hit here a couple of years ago, I saw a man interviewed on the local news. He lived in a trailer court and had been standing, naked as the day he was born, shaving in front of his medicine cabinet mirror. The winds ripped off the side of his mobile home, leaving him standing there shaken, but virtually unharmed. "They kept warning us," he said, "but I didn't believe it."

I've watched my children cram for a test or practice too late for a piano recital. They barely made a good showing approaching their responsibilities like this. I believe the race is run best in a sure and steady way.

A woman in England, bedridden for many years, watched as a bird built a nest in a tree outside her window. But it built the nest so low that she feared for its safety. Every day, as her little feathered friend structured the nest, the old lady kept warning, "Build a little higher!" She knew that the bird was likely to come to grief.

At last it laid eggs and hatched them. She watched, concerned, while the mother brought food for her little ones. Then one morning she saw nothing but scattered feathers. A cat!

"It would have been a kindness if I had torn her nest down the first day," she lamented.

This is what God does for us very often. He snatches things away before it is too late.

Many who have fallen would love to go back before that

time even for a brief moment. How differently they would guard their motives as they labored for the great end for which our Lord suffered and died, and for which we are now practicing, heaven.

Many people, even many churches, have forgotten that our real mission is to bring back the world to God. We are sometimes like the traveling salesman who gets so busy living it up that he forgets to sell his products—and loses his job. Our assignment is not to build a personal monument, but to lift up the name of the Son of the living God.

If we don't start now, it may soon be too late to join that great throng, blood-washed, faithfully toiling while they wait to join the mighty host above.

I like the illustration D. L. Moody used about being waterlogged.

A friend of his told him of seeing a vessel being towed along the River Mersey and into the Liverpool harbor. It appeared to be so heavily laden he wondered why it did not sink.

Pretty soon another large vessel came steaming into the harbor without any need for assistance.

The friend made inquiry and learned that the first vessel was waterlogged. That is, it had sprung a leak and sunk partially, making it hard to bring in.

Many Christians have become waterlogged. They have laden themselves down with too many treasures and it takes nearly the whole church to keep them afloat, to keep them from sinking into the world's riches. If we are not reaching the world, perhaps it is because we have more of the world in our hulls than we do of the grace and thoughts of God. We have too much earth and not enough heaven.

We get salvation as a free gift, but we have to work out

how we choose to live in relation to it. If you inherited a diamond mine, you would have to work it to make it profitable.

When Paul's life was threatened, he didn't flinch. He didn't write letters to defend himself, didn't debate on television or try to justify himself or his mistakes. Instead, he said he would do it all over again for God. His only regret was that he didn't start to serve God earlier, and that he had ever lifted his voice against the Lord.

I believe he went through the royal receiving line shouting, "Hallelujah! O my God! I bless Thee that I am in heaven at last!" His joy obliterated any remnants of earthly sorrow.

We cannot be selfish and unloving in one life and generous and loving in the next. The two lives are too closely blended, one a continuation of the other. We bring to heaven the same talents and tastes, desires and knowledge we had before. If these are not sufficiently pure and good, if our repentance is not heartfelt, then we may not receive all heaven is meant to be for us.

What would be the use of spending seventy years here pursuing certain knowledge and goals if, at death, all counts as nothing and we begin our heavenly lives on a different line of thought and study? Practice now. The more earnestly we follow the studies and duties of our lives of probation, the better fitted we shall be to carry them forward to completion and perfection there.

Several years ago *Guideposts* magazine carried Billy Kay Bothwell's story. She was a high school sophomore and for an English assignment wrote a story called "The Last Week of My Life."

In the paper she told how she would prepare for death if she knew she had one week to live: spending time with her family and friends, visiting the sick and shut-ins with her minister, spending time in the woods enjoying God's beautiful creation, and church on Sunday.

The paper was dated March 15. One week later, on March 22, she was killed in a car accident.

Jesus said, "Behold, I am coming quickly, and My reward is with Me" (Revelation 22:12). Now is the time to prepare.

One important rehearsal that I think is fun to invest in here is singing.

I have an old record album of Ethel Waters singing, "When the storms of life are raging, stand by me." Many times when prayer doesn't lift us out of the day's fog, a sacrifice of singing will.

In December 1985 a skilled surgeon successfully removed an English walnut-sized tumor from down inside my spinal column. The recovery was slow and painful. I am so grateful that I am now free from pain and able to walk from three to five miles a day.

I was not prepared, however, for what is known as "post-surgical letdown." When people used to tell me about depression I didn't understand the term. I do now. About five weeks after surgery a heavy, dark blanket descended on me and I could not lift it. I prayed. I walked the floor. I read the Psalms out loud. I was living in North Dakota and went outside in the zero temperatures to freeze it to death, but that unexplainable dark atmosphere squelched me down, down.

Then one day I sat at the piano. My fingers would hardly move, my mind would hardly perform. The words came from a weak, feeble voice, scratchy and helpless, but I sacrificed a song of praise. I sang, "Praise the name of Jesus, praise the name of Jesus. . . ."

Each verse got stronger. I began to feel elevated, like climbing a ladder one step at a time, up and out of the pit until I could see the light and feel the sun on my spirit's face!

Even if you can't sing well, begin worshiping God in song, rehearsing for the time when you will join that grand chorus and give Him praise for redeeming you out of sorrow into His glorious forever.

George Herbert (1593–1633) wrote of praising God:

Seven whole days, not one in seven, I will praise thee;
   in my heart, though not in heaven, I can raise thee.
Small it is in this poor sort to enroll thee;
   e'en eternity's too short to extol thee.

This morning at about ten before seven, the sun was coming up with a rosy glow and the mockingbirds in the holly bushes by my bedroom window were rehearsing, singing. I woke with a song in my heart, too, practicing for church this morning and for eternity where I will sing the way I've always wanted to sing.

I was born with a girl's body but a low, boy's singing voice. Nevertheless, I could sing fairly well until I had five nodes removed from my voice box. My voice doesn't sound as good as it did before surgery, but during my death experience I stood by the gates and joined the singers, and I sang as I feel it in my heart. That is one of the reasons I believe we will be able to do there what we have yearned to do here. We will be standing in the source of music and joy.

This completeness in us will even extend to areas of personality that we are working on as a sort of rehearsal for heaven. I'm learning, for instance, to control my short fuse. I tend to pop off quickly. I have a Scripture verse pasted on my mirror: "Set a watch, O Lord, before my mouth; keep the door of my lips" (Psalm 141:3, KJV). There I will finally *be* good and will desire only good things.

It's amazing how some things we don't focus on enough here, things like singing or building character, will be important there, and some things we think are so important here, certain cravings, will be without consequence there.

I was sitting in the Minneapolis airport early last fall when an attractive young woman offered me a cigarette.

"No thanks," I replied. "I'm too stingy to smoke. Too proud, too; don't want my breath bad or my teeth yellow." Then I laughed.

She smiled in return. "Oh, I see. I thought you were going to be like my mom and preach at me. Tell me," she said. "Give me one good reason why I shouldn't smoke."

I thought to myself, *I've already given you two!* But out loud I said, "I guess that sign says it all." I pointed to the letters that stood out above the jetway door: *No Smoking Beyond*.

She laughed and said, "If I can't smoke in heaven I guess I won't go! I'm telling you the same as I told the doctor when I went to get something for my cough. I'd rather die than quit cigarettes."

Now I certainly don't advocate smoking, but that habit—even for someone as addicted as that young woman—will be so insignificant that once you step into that glorious place, you'll never think of it again. "Old things are passed away; behold, all things are become new" (2 Corinthians 5:17, KJV). This is a Scripture promise for the new believer here, and it pertains to the new arrival there, too. I believe that some self-indulgences we think we can't live without here will be discarded like a menstrual pad.

Pray for an understanding heart to help people along

the way to overcome sin and discard their hang-ups. Pray to become intensely spiritual that you may become genuinely human. Exhort the weak along the road. The angels are strong to minister because they worship and bless and obey God. We humans can have supernatural strength if we follow their examples along our journey. We have the power of life in our tongues (Proverbs 18:21). There are no dead words.

Not long ago I saw the movie *Cross Creek* about Marjorie Kinnan Rawlings, a Florida writer and author of *The Yearling*. She loved the sky, the water, the earth. She said, "I was a part of the earth before I became a part of the womb."

We were created from the earth, belong to time, and are headed for eternity!

Several years ago, when I first started writing, I cried mother tears while I interviewed a young fellow who had just broken both wrists during a basketball game. Looking up at his mother and me with a big smile, he cheered, "We won!"

What a victory cry we will give when we stand at those gates knowing we have given it our all, we have rehearsed and are now ready. "We made it!" we'll shout. "We won!"

In the words of this old song:

I am watching for the coming of the glad millennial day
When our blessed Lord shall come and take his waiting
   bride away.
Oh, my heart is filled with rapture as I labor, watch,
   and pray
For our Lord is coming back to earth again.

9

How Is Heaven?

Many jokes come to me through my mailbox, a number of them bantering about St. Peter at the heavenly gates screening applicants. One man wrote: ''There is no prejudice there. Here's all it takes to get in: The Catholics just have to spell God, and the Protestants just have to spell Albuquerque.''

In one sense heaven is found very easily: by believing in Jesus Christ.

In another sense this is not so easy because it means giving yourself to Him totally, allowing yourself forevermore to be under His Lordship and sovereignty. Yet you will never find a kinder or truer master. And you will find no other way to heaven but by believing on His name. Entrance to heaven is not acquired by our works or accomplishments, lest we would be able to boast about ourselves. It is given as a free gift of grace in response to a heart of faith. (See Ephesians 2:8–9.)

Jesus came to make life easy. He never hurried, never worried. He lived with the answer because He was the answer. Many churches have complicated Christianity. They have become as practical to eternal life as a silk hat in a hurricane or a clown at a funeral. Some have become religious theaters, drama centers, rehearsed religion instead of reality where a person can simply find the door to eternal life and be born again.

As Jack Hayford has expressed, the Lord draws us back regularly to simplicity. We must avoid the superficial, the fads.

Just as you can have only one earthly father, there is only one way to your heavenly Father, and that is through Jesus. The same rule applies for getting through life as getting through Mammoth Cave: Stay close to your guide. Jesus' life was not a performance but a process, as ours should be.

We must resolve that our churches are not Hollywood and our leaders are not movie stars. People struggling for security, survival, and salvation will look to us if we are real, if we are sincere.

Jesus spent a great deal of time teaching how we must become like little children if we are to inherit the Kingdom of God.

I love the fable *The Little Prince* by Antoine de Saint-Exupery. The little prince asks a question and the Answerer replies hurriedly, "No, I don't believe anything. I answered you with the first thing that came into my head. Don't you see—I am very busy with matters of consequence."

The little prince stared. "Matters of consequence? You talk just like the grown-ups!"

For heaven's sake, quit acting like an adult!

I spoke for a Lutheran Conference on the Holy Spirit in Madison, Wisconsin. It was held in a Catholic convent and I stayed in one of the sisters' rooms. The floor was plain tile, no carpet. There was a chest, one desk, a twin-sized bed, and no mirror. You would be surprised how much time we could save if there were no mirrors! You wouldn't worry so much about how you look, just how you feel. The idea was that those women were there for one purpose: learning how to get people to heaven.

John Sherrill, although a religion writer, confessed how years ago he finally realized that the people who were busiest with religion were sometimes farthest from the real, life-changing heart of it—himself included. One day, while facing cancer surgery, he removed the roadblocks of logic and quit approaching Jesus with his mind. Suddenly he said out loud, "I'm making the leap by faith. I believe in Jesus." His life was never the same again.

Personally, I believe that after being born again, after Jesus' blood has washed away our sins of the past, we should at the first opportunity be baptized. This is the public confession of the personal inward work of grace.

Some of my family have been baptized inside the sanctuary of the church, but, since Jesus was baptized in a river, I asked to be baptized outside by immersion. Baptism is a symbol that represents Jesus' death, burial, and resurrection. It represents that fact that you were dead in trespasses and sins and have buried the old life and risen to walk a new life.

In many churches babies are sprinkled. I believe this is more of a promissory dedication of the parents to teach their children the precepts of the faith. I would recommend that when a child chooses to receive eternal life at an age of accountability that he or she also choose to be immersed.

Perhaps you are reading now and you have been baptized and confirmed, but were in such a hurry that you did not receive all that God intended you to have. Pause and believe. Trust and receive with childlike faith. Jesus said that unless we receive the Kingdom of God as a little child we shall not enter in (Mark 10:15).

There is nothing quite like the faith—or imagination—of a child! I have received letters from children who are excited about heaven, but worried about how they'll get there, especially if they are taken up in the Rapture. They imagine dangling up in the sky or floating along without a good foothold.

I write back to tell them that death or the Rapture will happen as quickly as the lightning flashes from the east to the west (Matthew 24:27) or as quick as a wink (1 Corinthians 15:52). Jesus will come and take us so fast we won't know it has happened until we are suddenly there. It's just like the way we can't detect the exact second we fall asleep at night; it's quick.

The Bible says that during the Rapture two will be sleeping in one bed; one will be taken, the other left. It will happen before they even realize it. Likewise, two will be working the field and the one who is ready will be taken and the other will not. I can just see a Dakota tractor go into automatic pilot when some good man takes off for heaven!

Evelyn Pacadio wrote me about a dream she had of quick transport to heaven. She saw her family transported and saw wheels whirring rapidly. She believes these are the wheels spoken of in Ezekiel where Jesus is the wheel in the middle of a wheel. (Maybe there will be holy bikers in heaven!)

I believe it is possible to decide how you depart according to the way you have lived. I want to tell you about our old friend Noel Perkin. He was national missions secretary/

treasurer for the General Council of the Assemblies of God
for many years. My maiden name was Perkins and he
used to tease me, an unknown, that my name had the "s"
for distinction. He was that modest in everything he did.
A big man can afford to be magnanimous.

One Sunday I was embarrassed to arrive late for the
church services. I was slipping into the children's church
entrance when I caught sight of Noel Perkin arriving late,
too. He patted my back and, grinning, said, "Now that the
saints are all seated, shall *we* go in?"

Noel was over ninety when his time came. He told our
friend Gary McGee that he was going to die on Wednesday. "I have prayed that the Lord not take me at home,"
he said, "since my wife is in a wheelchair and would feel
helpless to assist me and would have bad memories in our
house."

On Wednesday morning he knelt beside his bed, read a
passage from his Bible, underlined it, and left a note that
they should use it for his funeral. He then left the house to
go make some hospital visitations. He opened the car door
and, perhaps feeling faint, knelt and lay his head on his
arms on the front seat. Then he simply slept. What a way
to go!

Ann Moreton was an airline hostess married to a florist.
Fred was suffering with an inoperable malignancy. He
prayed, "Lord, I want to die in dignity." He had lived that
way, reading his Bible, giving away lots of flowers, so why
not?

Ann was leaving the hospital one evening when he told
her, "Go home and get a nap. Be sure you come back by
midnight."

That evening she was at home and started to write some

letters when suddenly she felt two hands on her shoulders pushing her toward the door. She followed the nudge and hurried to the hospital. There she greeted him. "Hello, Freddie. I've come to stay with you."

"That's fine, sweetie," he said in a natural tone of voice, "for I'm dying."

He breathed a few shallow breaths, then said, "God, I'm coming." It was over easily. Ann said that everything in the room appeared to be in "soft focus."

Fred's spirit had grown too large for his earth body. The doctors said, "We've never seen anyone go in such an open, clear-eyed way."

Ann said that after seeing him suffer for two years all she could do was lay her head down on the table and rest.

Bobbie Morrison's mother was dying of cancer. Bobbie was with her mother when she said, "Jesus is at the door. Let Him in." Bobbie could tell by the look on her mother's face that she really saw something. Though Bobbie could not detect anything unusual she said she knew by the atmosphere in the room that they were not alone.

Bobbie hugged her mother and said, "Don't leave me now that we're just getting to know each other."

Her mother said, "I have to go." And she did so, totally unafraid.

Thank God for His eternal plan in which we can redeem the time lost on earth.

Coni Perez wrote this from Los Angeles:

My three sisters and I all felt compelled at the same time to visit my mother's hospital room. I knew she was dying when we arrived. I prayed that the Lord would send angels to attend her and make it easy for her. We suddenly felt an unbelievable power in the room. The solid line appeared on her heart monitor, [then] her eyes were open again. She *ooohed* at the wonders she was seeing, cocked her head to one side as if in extreme attention, smiled the greatest, grandest, broadest smile, lifted both arms straight upward, and was gone.

The time is drawing near when the angels will shout and sing, "Hallelujah! The Lord omnipotent reigneth!" I feel that the Lord will invite us to a royal banquet given by Himself in honor of the last arrivals. I can hardly wait to sing the Doxology—"Praise God from whom all blessings flow. . . ." I can just see the many rows of banquet tables, covered in white linen, gorgeously furnished with golden and crystal goblets, fruits from the tree of life served by angelic waiters. We will lack nothing.

I believe we will have dinner music sung by special singers from earth and perhaps violinists strolling by, great musicians hitting perfect pitches. No untuned strings, no self-consciousness, everyone doing his best for Him and us.

Perhaps David the psalmist will stand and sing from the book of Revelation: "God shall wipe away all tears from their eyes; and there shall be no more death, neither sorrow, nor crying, neither shall there be any more pain: for the former things are passed away" (Revelation 21:4, KJV)

And He that sits upon the throne may stand and announce: "Behold, I am making all things new. . . . I am the Alpha and the Omega, the beginning and the end. I will give to the one who thirsts from the spring of the water of life without cost. He who overcomes shall inherit

these things, and I will be his God and he will be My son"
(Revelation 21:5–7). Then we will shout, "Hallelujah!"

Daniel may be sitting next to you and lean over and
whisper, "What a moment this is for me! While I was on
earth I saw Him as the Ancient of Days long before His
Advent by the virgin Mary. His garment was white as
snow and the hair of His head was like pure wool. In the
revelations God gave me I saw Him sitting on that very
throne. Look, His throne is like a fiery flame. He is now
Judge and the books are finally opening."

All things will be made new and we can be there to see
them. If you have found the way, don't let anything cause
you to stray from the course. There is no greater treasure
on this earth than the pathway to heaven. And if you
remain faithful, He will look at you at the end of it with the
light of His love and say, "Welcome."

10

The Banking System of Eternity

Every creature, I believe, is born with the desire not only to survive but to thrive.

Perhaps I think this because of the games my Aunt Pearl, whom I then called Pib, and I used to play. Since we were close to the same age, and since we grew up before the days of television we manufactured games and played pretend all day long, usually having to do with lives of luxury.

We would place two chairs on the flat top roof of my grandparents' cow shed and sit up there dressed regally in high heels, purses with stacks of play money, wearing plastic jewelry and pretending to reign as British royalty. We were queens over our domain, which was three acres including a blackberry patch, a cornfield, a ditch and creek, a cow and a calf, and a grape arbor. Dad Burns' old Ford was our limousine.

At school we skipped rope while singing, "Rich man, poor man, beggar man, thief, doctor, lawyer, merchant, chief." The word you were saying when you missed indicated the profession of the man you would marry. Naturally, we were not disappointed when "rich man" was the choice!

In the midst of this fanciful living, faith was instilled in us from the bassinet during family altar and daily devotions. We actually prayed that our dolls would come to life and we had faith to believe that God would give us anything we asked. When our dolls didn't start living we put mustard in their diapers and kept mothering them. I'm glad God reserves the answers to some prayers for a more appropriate time. At age ten we were not quite prepared for motherhood!

Through the years Pearl and I have overcome many hurdles and faced many storms and have found God faithful. Our childhood dreams of riches have changed into the longing for the inheritance waiting for us in heaven. It is there that all of our dreams will come true. The investments in the Bank of Eternity will meet every need and every desire.

How do we determine what inheritances are waiting for each of us? How do we transfer funds into eternity's bank? How do we get assets from planet earth to planet heaven?

Our shares in the Bank of Eternity are based on the investments we made while living here on earth. And the best way to make investments in our heavenly account is by investing in others. When someone gives to others in this life in the name of Jesus, it's like putting it into the Lord's hand to invest—not for 5¼% but 100%, one hundredfold! Even one cup of water, given in His name, will transfer for great yield of reward there.

Jesus explained how our service here reaps rewards there when He said that the one who would be the greatest must serve (Matthew 23:11). The Bible also says that believers will receive crowns, which will be converted to positions of rulership. By serving in a humble and lowly fashion here, we will rule with Christ in eternity.

I received a professionally printed appeal from a male

hairstylist begging me to contribute $1,000 so he could enter a contest in France. That same day I got a letter from a retired couple, he a minister, she a nurse, asking the name of a young woman I had told them about who had cancer. They wanted to offer her a home, care, love, and medical ministry—in effect, to become the parents she did not have. What a contrast!

If the hairstylist makes it to heaven, his halo will outshine his hairdo; if he goes to hell, his curly perm may burn. But that couple is investing in a person who will live as a witness to their love forever.

Ralph Wilkerson tells of a missionary friend of his who built several churches in the Philippines. One of his first was in Manila in a huge evangelistic center able to accommodate thousands. Then God called him into the bush. How did he set about to introduce the pagans to Christ?

First he built his house on a path where a tribe passed regularly going to the springs for water. He tried preaching, but got no response. Then he decided to quit preaching and start "practicing Jesus." The next day when an elderly man came by he gave him a cup of water from his well and said simply, "I give you this drink in Jesus' name."

Before long, more of the tribesmen were stopping for the free water. Soon they were not just drinking natural water, but the Water of Life, Christ. Now the tribe is coming to know Jesus.

People don't care how much you know until they know how much you care.

I have made it a practice to invest in people anonymously as much as possible. It is fun to give this way in the name of the Lord and, most important, God is honored. Remember that those recording angels are excellent bookkeepers and gauge your motive as much as your gift. Am I doing it through love, or to show off my goodness, my charity, my "spirituality," my wealth?

God says He is not unrighteous to forget our work and the love we have shown toward His name in ministering to the saints (Hebrews 6:10) and we know that where our treasure is, our heart will be also (Luke 12:34). If we throw our hearts into serving Jesus, eventually our bodies will follow our treasures to heaven.

Some people's main talent seems to be making money. This is to be a means of service, stewardship of what God has given them. And it is not merely the amount that one gives that matters, but one's attitude.

My grandparents rented a house on a hillside west of Terre Haute for sixty years. They rented it most of those years from a miserly landlady. She complained that her husband would eat a whole potato if she would fix it for him. She died alone of malnutrition with $1,800 under her mattress, too stingy to pay someone to go and do her grocery shopping for her.

Dr. Arnot gives this apt illustration regarding our lives and eternity's treasure.

A ship bearing a company of immigrants is driven off-course and wrecked on an island. They have a good stock of food, plenty of seed, fine soil, and spring and summer ahead of them.

Before plans are made to fell trees and plant crops, they explore and find a gold mine. They begin to dig right away and labor day after day and month after month. They acquire great heaps of gold, but spring is now past and not a field has been cleared, not a grain of seed put into the ground.

Summer comes and their wealth increases, but the stock of food grows small. Soon they are eating the seed. In the fall they find that their heaps of gold are worthless in the face of famine.

They rush to fell trees, till the ground, and sow the seed, but it is too late. Winter has come and the seed rots in the ground. They die of want in the midst of their treasure.

This earth is like that island, with eternity the ocean around it. On this shore we have the living seed, but we are constantly enticed to spend our time and energy elsewhere. Once winter overtakes us in our useless toil, however, we are without the Bread of Life and are lost. As Christians we should value all the more the home that holds the treasure we desire and should remember that we invest in eternity by the way we live now.

Ministers would not have to urge people to live for heaven if their treasures were up there; their hearts would already be there.

I talked with a former prostitute from a Southern city. She said, "I made a lot of money by evil. Now that God has redeemed me through Jesus I have transferred my funds into the hands of the preachers I used to hate as religious fanatics." Your money goes where your heart is.

Mrs. William Booth, wife of the founder of the Salvation Army, told her daughter, "The moments of opportunity here will be worth countless millions there. The inestimable privileges of time will make us ashamed that we did not take heaven's banking system more seriously."

Peter said that those who remain sure of their calling will have "the entrance into the eternal kingdom of our Lord and Savior Jesus Christ . . . abundantly supplied" (2 Peter 1:10–11).

When Carl's first wife died he asked that in lieu of flowers that would wither, gifts of money be given to their daughter, Connie, so she could go to Bible school. Now, with three children of her own, with that love gift and a grant, she is doing just that. The going wasn't always easy, but she persevered through the difficult times and is enjoying her reward.

We might think of this earth as college training for the forever life. "So teach us to number our days, that we may apply our hearts unto wisdom" (Psalm 90:12, KJV).

Who knows the wealth and position for which God is preparing us? Even if He is subjecting us to painful training now, we shouldn't rebel. His plans are always good and every adversity we face will be used to help prepare us for an eternity with Him. I think that the more we are able to overcome our trials with grace and humility, the more we will find waiting for us in eternity's bank.

God has always had a remnant throughout the centuries willing to pay the price of spiritual maturity. As a man seeks treasure, so the Lord seeks followers like these. "For the eyes of the Lord run to and fro throughout the whole earth, to show himself strong in the behalf of them whose heart is perfect" (2 Chronicles 16:9, KJV).

We will find that the wealthy ones in heaven were first servants here on earth (Mark 10:43–44). They are the ones who gave their time to fold stacks of Sunday school papers, or tend to the church nursery, or chauffeur the elderly. The quiet person of prayer will likely be met with a thirty-piece angelic brass band, while some who have been more showy in their approach to Christianity will be less heralded. We may forget some of the little things we have done, but it is all recorded and rewards are waiting for us. If our small deeds are rewarded, what must be the benefit for larger sacrifices?

Do not miss them at any cost, for they must be wonderful. In the book of Revelation Jesus says, "He who overcomes, I will grant to him to sit down with Me on My throne, as I also overcame and sat down with My Father on His throne" (Revelation 3:21).

Now is the time to give our best. Attain our highest for Him here with all diligence. Work hard. Make every effort for others. Be earnest. "Those who have insight will shine brightly like the brightness of the expanse of heaven, and those who lead the many to righteousness, like the stars forever and ever" (Daniel 12:3).

All who believe in Jesus will go to heaven, but as I understand it we will be assigned to different locations or planes. Just as one star differs from another star in glory (1 Corinthians 15:41), all will have mansions, but some will be grander than others. All will serve, but some in higher positions according to their obedience on earth. All will be happy, but some will be happier.

If only we could understand the glories of heaven we would lead very different lives, seeking to be ready for it. Our imaginations cannot fathom even a small part of how grand and real heaven is.

When the steamship *Central America* went down, several hundred miners, returning with fortunes in gold, lost their lives. It's good to have gold, but it makes a bad life-preserver. Riches can be a weight that crushes us down to hell, that drowns us in the sea of life.

As John Milton said, there is nothing that makes men rich and strong but that which they carry inside of them. True wealth is of the heart, not of the hand.

Make yourself a private inventory sheet and list your goals. How many of them are spiritual, eternal goals and how many are temporary, material goals? This may help you see how much you are investing in the Bank of Heaven.

Look at the story Jesus told of the rich man and Lazarus.

The rich man looks over his marble balcony at Lazarus the beggar and commands his dogs, "Take hold of him."

The dogs go at the beggar with a terrible bark, then stop and yawn. They frisk about him and put their soft, healing tongues to his sores, driving away the flies, relieving the sting of wounds that have no salve or bandage. Lazarus is friends with the rich man's dogs.

Then Lazarus dies. Two men dig a hole and lower him into a pauper's grave. But it isn't Lazarus they bury. It is only his sores. Yonder goes Lazarus with an angel on the right and an angel on the left. They carry him to heaven, talking, praising, and rejoicing.

Abraham stands at the gate and throws his arms around the newcomer. Lazarus has his own house, his own robes, his own banquet table and chariot; and that poor sickly carcass of his that the overseers of the town dumped in the potter's field will come up at the call of the archangel straight and pure and healthy, corruption having become incorruption.

Now, back in the city, the dead body of the rich man lies in state on an Oriental rug. He is carried out of his splendid room through the streets where long eulogies are given. A long procession files to his burial place.

The rich man who had all the wines he could drink now asks for plainer beverage: He just wants water. Not a cupful, not a teaspoonful, but just "one drop" and he cannot get it. He looks and sees Lazarus, the man he sicked his dogs on, resting joyfully with Abraham.

He calls to the patriarch and begs for Lazarus to put his finger in water and let him lick it off. Once Lazarus asked for crumbs from his feast; now the rich man begs for a drop of water from Lazarus' banquet.

Poor as he can be, he has eaten the last quail's wing. He has broken the last rind of the last pomegranate. The rich lord has become the pauper. Now he sits at the gate, watching the heavenly festivities with longing.

The social gulf that separated Lazarus from the rich man in this world is not nearly so great as the spiritual chasm that now separates them forever. He begs Abraham to send Lazarus to his brothers to warn them before it is too late for them, too.

But as Abraham tells him, most people are preoccupied with their comforts, and even if someone did come back from the dead (and people have) they would not listen.

Jesus did not by this parable condemn the acquisition of wealth, but its wrongful application. A man of wealth is not necessarily a sinner. Solomon and David were both rich, as was Job. And we're glad for the great philanthropists who give their gifts to colleges, churches, and hospitals for education, ministry, and relief for the poor.

Jesus had in mind the haughty, vain, and self-sufficient rich who, like the Pharisees, use their wealth to oppress the less fortunate and to make a vulgar show of their advantages. It is this pride, pomp, and circumstance that leads men away from God.

Jesus is the Messiah and will return for His believers to take them to His heavenly Kingdom. He said that many would try to show us signs of His appearing, but to regard none of them, for they are intended to catch the weak and lead them to destruction.

When the Son of Man comes in judgment it will be sudden like lightning. Just as it was in the days of Noah when the floods came to swallow up the world after the people refused to repent of their perversions, just as it was when Sodom was consumed for its offenses, so will it be again when Jesus comes and reveals His power.

In that day, those who have not prepared themselves, as did Noah and Lot by prayer and repentance, will be destroyed. The good in family, social, and business relations will be separated from the bad. The evil will be delivered up for punishment; the righteous will go to their reward.

How can you multiply your investments in heaven's bank? Sell what you have and give to the poor. Don't be high-minded or trust in riches. Do good works. Build for yourself a trust fund in heaven and you will find that He helps you out here on earth, too.

In fact, God advances some of the interest on the eternal benefits now, with the principal still intact in the Bank of Eternity. Some of the assets are love, peace, joy, eternal youth and energy, forever life. The Scripture says to give and it will be given to you, good measure, pressed down, shaken together, and running over (Luke 6:38). And that's just for starters. The principal that has been building and the interest that has been accruing are awaiting your arrival in heaven.

It seems that we *can* take it with us! Everything we give away we keep. We have converted it into heavenly currency, exchanged paper money for wealth that cannot burn or fade. "The generous man will be prosperous. . . . He who trusts in his riches will fall" (Proverbs 11:25, 28), or, as the King James Version puts it: "There is that withholdeth more than is meet, but it tendeth to poverty. The liberal soul shall be made fat" (Proverbs 24–25).

Ask the Lord in private prayer what you can do this week for the church or someone in need, if you want a sure investment!

11

What's Forever For?

You have undoubtedly heard the expressions "You mean there's more?" and "I never dreamed that . . ." and "Have you ever . . . ?"

Upon our arrival at heaven's golden shore I'm sure we'll exclaim that we had no idea there could be so much more to living, that we had only begun to know the rudiments of life at its fullest and living at its best, that there is more than we had ever imagined.

I can't wait to introduce John to our daughter April. If the Rapture occurs before I die I hope the Lord will cause me to zigzag a little on the way up to meet Erika and Ryan, our grandchildren, and meet John with one on each hand! Then I want to walk over to my mother and let her see her great-grandchildren.

Carl feels the same way. His grandchildren are scattered from North Dakota to North Carolina. We'll have plenty of time there to play with our grandchildren.

Have you ever wondered what we'll do for all of eternity? I can assure you there will be no monotony in heaven. There will also be no pressure because we will not sense the passing of time. It will be impossible for us to fail. Everything we touch will succeed. My dad says he wants forever to make up to Mother for the years on earth that he expected too much of her. She was never strong and died young trying to please everyone as mother, wife, pianist, teacher, even substitute preacher when he had to miss church for some reason.

I imagine that any writer who has ever received a manuscript rejection notice, marked with an X, will want to visit the "Acceptance Department."

I'm sure that many performers will be in the spotlight on "Request Night." Remember camp meeting when you couldn't get enough of the good singing? I think I'll request that Gordon Matheny and the Paino Brothers sing their old numbers "Looking for a City" and "The Stone Hewn Out of the Mountain."

Maybe you have always wanted to learn to play a piano yourself, or a harp. If you so desire, you could probably sign up for music lessons from King David or Bach. They will have plenty of time, forever, in fact, to teach and you to learn. There will be no lack of talent there, either. That place will lack nothing.

I'm sure that Carl will sign up for classes with St. Paul in biblical studies and church history.

And women will finally receive deserved recognition. Generations past have not always recognized the talents of women. I believe that God passes out talent without stopping to examine sex organs to see if the person is male or female.

Brenda is a music major and teaches piano. She is conscientious about copyrights and giving credit to whom credit is due. Recently she wrote me about some new music she had tracked down:

"You're familiar with the composer Robert Schumann. It seems that his wife, Clara, was a composer, too. Before she married she was considered one of the world's greatest pianists and did a lot of composing herself. (Chopin asked her to perform his music because she did it better than anyone else.) She wrote only a few things during her marriage and Robert was critical of most of it. She bore him eight children (five of whom lived) and edited most of his compositions. When he died she taught piano lessons and her mother helped her raise the children.

"I also picked up a collection of compositions by Mendelssohn's sister Fanny. Musicologists are starting to think that Fanny wrote some of what her brother published under his own name, for example, some of his 'Songs without Words.' "

There is no prejudice among angels. What a relief!

Any mistreatment of women and all other records—good and bad—will be accurate for forever.

It's amazing when traveling how often I deplane to comments or questions about bad news around the country. I like to smile and answer, "I stand behind not the fifth amendment but Philippians 4:8: Whatsoever things are lovely, of *good* report, think on these things."

Aren't you glad there will be no more gory news details on TV at 5:30 every afternoon? Although I've often surmised that if Jesus came at 5:40 my husband would miss the Rapture! The evening news is a *must* with Carl.

There will be no misunderstandings there. I've tried to adopt my grandfather's definition of maturity: Suffer without complaining, be misunderstood without explaining. That's hard, but the records will be straightened out there. We'll have our day in court.

I saw a vivid example of how we can misjudge our fellow man one Sunday morning when I was quite small. This was before cars had automatic turn signals; you used your left arm.

Dad was driving our old Hudson. We were running late for church and the man in front of us was driving quite slowly. Then he turned quickly to the left without signaling in order to get a newspaper from a boy barking "Sunday *News*!" on the corner.

As Dad braked to a halt, he remarked, "He could have caused a wreck! How did he ever get a license without learning hand signals?"

When the man stepped out of his car we saw that there was no sleeve on the left side of his shirt, only a stump of an arm. My father was quite chagrined to have judged him and I learned a valuable lesson.

Last week Carl and I took a break from work and headed for the beach for an hour. We saw an old lady trying to cross the street holding a bag. She slid on a rock, turned her ankle, and flung apples all over the curb. Carl stopped the car and I ran over to help her out of the traffic.

She hung onto my neck and asked pitifully, "Is this what old means?" I had to tell her that it happens to us all here, but there is no "old" in heaven. She cried and replied, "Then let's go there."

We will have forever for joys and accomplishments.

I believe we will have total recall, no mental limitations. I've read that psychiatrists say we use only about ten percent of our mental ability. Everything there will be 100 percent. John 14:26 promises that the Holy Spirit will teach us all things and bring all things to our remembrance.

There will be no power failure in heaven to wipe out a morning's work on your word processor during hurricane season. No tornadoes, either.

The thief on the cross believed in Jesus at the last minute. The Lord did not have time to teach him anything, but assured him, "Today you will be with Me in paradise."

That man will have forever to learn about Jesus and to enjoy heaven. If you want a headstart, read the Bible and start singing meaningful songs. It's certain we won't be bored, twirling halos like hula hoops there. What job opportunities to teach the newcomers! Have you tried to tell someone something who already knows everything? I hate to try to feed a kid who isn't hungry. I want to teach people who haven't heard it all, unspoiled, thirsty learners.

What fun to see relatives we haven't seen in ages and those our parents talked about but we were born too late to know. I've always wanted to meet several Bible characters. I want to know what Samson saw in Delilah that caused him to sell his strength. I want to talk to Jonah about being in that whale's stomach.

I won't be afraid of breaking my neck when I learn to waterski on just one ski. I may even walk on the water. The Scripture tells us the river is a sea like glass. There is no drowning, no death, no risk involved.

There will be no more worrying about the affairs of the nations, either. The destiny of the universe, including the planet earth, will be under the jurisdiction of God from His throne in heaven. Romans 13:1 says that "the powers that be are ordained of God" (kjv). Daniel 2:21 says that God removes kings and sets up kings.

I'm looking forward to being free from worry about my children. Mother used to say that when your children are babies you worry about their safety. When they are growing up your worry increases as you watch them learn to drive, dive, date. When they marry you worry about their being properly respected. When they're safely adjusted in their marriages you worry about the inexperienced way they rear your grandchildren!

Even though I pray the Scripture "I know whom I have believed and am persuaded that he is able to keep that which I've committed unto him against *that day*," I still have a tender, overconcerned heart. I promised John I'd bring them "home" to him.

Judy Provost wrote me from California, "I have just lost my partner. We had such a good life . . . taking walks by the ocean. I can't believe it's over."

It isn't. Those hikes will be continued in a lovelier place. I've been to California and to heaven and, believe me, the most beautiful part of California—or anywhere else—is shabby by comparison.

Uncle Arch Brown, my great-uncle, used to sing this old hymn:

> When I take my vacation in heaven
> What a wonderful time that will be,
> Hearing concerts by the heavenly chorus
> And the face of the Savior I'll see.
>
> Sitting down by the banks of the river
> 'Neath the shade of the evergreen tree,
> I shall rest from my burdens forever.
> Won't you spend your vacation with me?

If you want to travel, that's what forever is for. Read the description of the Garden of Eden. This is only a transplant from the original paradise. Can you imagine touring cliffs, mountains, vales, and glens? The fields will be teeming with harvest, the valleys spread out before you.

Not a drop of sweat will be needed to gather these fields of golden harvest. No curse there, no weeds, thorns, or briars. Everything grows in heaven without human toil, yet we will be employed to gather the great harvests and the labor is a kind of picnic for joy.

There will be plenty of room for the millions who will be born again and come there with hope, joy, expectation. I have fond memories of drinking from the unpolluted streams of North and South Dakota right after the snows melted. What cooool refreshment! Think of drinking from the river proceeding out of the throne of God. You could dip a golden goblet into it, drink, and never thirst again. How invigorating it will be to feel the joyful glow of youth, never to feel tired, weary, or old again after drinking the water of life (Revelation 22:1).

I believe that we can go from place to place either in the air or the solid foundations of the celestial country. "But there the glorious Lord will be unto us a place of broad rivers and streams; wherein shall go no galley with oars" (Isaiah 33:21, KJV). Can you imagine a boat ride powered by the Holy Spirit's energy, no noisy motors, but heaven's energy of light and power? Perhaps on the shore can be heard angelic groups singing and praising God night and day.

I believe we will hear old and new songs. I believe that many of the inspired songs we hear now on earth were inspired first in heaven and we will sing them there. There will be concerts perhaps daily and the Temple will be filled with the smoke from the glory of God and from His power (Revelation 15:8). Trumpeters will play and hosts sing:

Holy, holy, holy! Lord God Almighty!
All Thy works shall praise Thy Name, in earth, and sky,
    and sea;
Holy, holy, holy, merciful and mighty!
God in Three Persons, blessed Trinity.

Reginald Heber (1783–1826)

We will never tire of study. Much will be taught just by observation as we take in at our leisure all the parts of His heavenly Kingdom.

We will never lack for social pleasures and enjoyments for there is no clashing of duty with inclination, no unfulfilled desires, no vain striving for the unattainable in that life.

I would not be surprised if some of us whose friends or relatives were builders find that they have built us a home on the water, if we like water sports, with bluebirds singing in the overhanging willow nearby and hummingbirds darting in the flowery windowboxes.

Many precious hours will be spent with our families that we did not have time for before, going with each other to our various fields of labor and ministry, helping instruct those come lately into the new life with little or no knowledge of the heavenly.

I imagine there will be talks, lectures, sharing times when we can hear Martin Luther, John Wesley, George Whitefield; when we can enjoy the happy presence of the virgin Mary and hear her tell of the visit by the angel Gabriel and the events that followed. Perhaps we will hear a pep talk (not that we'll need it) from Peter, the energetic one.

And imagine the joy of having the Word, the Bethlehem

Baby, the Son of God now walking and talking as friend with friend. What ecstasy!

At some point we will see Jesus sitting on a white horse. It must be some gallant steed. When He was on earth they borrowed a donkey for Him. But there He will be called by the whole universe Faithful and True (Revelation 19:11).

Now we know in part. There we will see things as they really are. He may take us on a field trip to show us how to make a rainbow or share the ingredients to form a star.

Here we usually receive an inheritance at the death of someone close to us. There we will have our heavenly Father *and* an inheritance! My earthly dad will be there beside me, too. That's a piece of joy. He'll be whistling each morning as he did at 5:00 A.M. on our farm, happy to meet the sunrise, loving his work, thinking about heaven.

We will get there what we lost out on here. I recall the words to another old song: "Leave the unknown future in the Master's hands; whether sad or joyful, Jesus understands."

Look around at people you work with or family members who are not looking for that blessed hope, His return. They are spiritually blind, uninformed of the Good News, crippled with feeble knees that haven't bent in prayer for years. They have no faith but I believe we can *give them ours* by praying for them.

Look at the New Testament story of the crippled man who had no strength or faith of his own. Four friends carried him by their faith, took off a section of the roof in a crowded house, and dropped his cot down into the living room in front of Jesus. That man was actually healed because he borrowed someone else's faith.

We can get more faith if we give ours away because we

know the Source! Bring those unbelieving people to Jesus and you will have sheaves to lay at the Master's feet. You will receive your crown and hear Him say, "Well done, thou good and faithful servant."

I was amazed by a story of servanthood of two women living in India a number of years ago who took in abandoned or orphaned children. One of them, an American who was grieving over a broken engagement, had thrown herself into missionary work.

One day they heard a knock on the door early in the morning. A man was standing there with a little bundle in his hands. He said he had gone to the outer edge of the village where a dung heap served as the toilet for the village when he saw something stir in the leaves by a tree. He brushed the leaves away and found a newborn girl. Girls in that culture were not considered worth keeping.

He asked the two women if they would take the child, and they did. They had ten nursing babies at that time and, as one of the women remarked, "We didn't get much sleep, but our prayer life was incredible."

They reared the girl until she was seven years old and a wealthy couple from New Delhi adopted her.

One day, years later, the two women received a letter from London with a picture of the girl, now grown. She wrote that she had been musically talented and her adoptive parents had sent her to the London Conservatory of Music. She became a concert pianist and the picture showed her at tea in Buckingham Palace. Today she is married to an executive and holds Bible studies in her home.

It's a long way from a broken engagement to ministry in India. And it's a long way from a dung heap to Buckingham Palace. But if we let the power of God use us here, we will find that we have all of forever to enjoy His good pleasure.

You may have your passport in order and have your ticket in hand, but to take off you must go to the airport. Scripture recommends that we "not [forsake] the assembling of ourselves together . . . as [we] see the day approaching" (Hebrews 10:25, KJV). Find believers to worship with until He appears.

He's coming again. It is the climax of the entire Bible. We're not talking about just the Rapture; we're talking about revelation. We're not talking just about meeting Him in the air; we're talking about coming back to the earth to reign with Him. We're not only talking about His coming for the saints; we're talking about His coming with the saints. We're not talking about His coming to comfort and protect; we're talking about His coming to conquer and rule.

No wonder John exploded with praise at the end of the book of Revelation! No wonder he cried out, "Even so, come, Lord Jesus!"

What's forever for? It's for everything and for a long time. And we'll enjoy every eternal moment of it.

12

Going Home

When college students have marked the last days of the semester off the calendar, have just answered the last question on the final exam, and are running toward their cars, which are packed and filled with gas, that's anticipation!

Christians have been marking their calendars, too, waiting for the glorious return of Jesus. We'll be going home. The Grand Finale.

A book by Sir William Barrett published in 1926 contained many near-death experiences, and the visions of those who died. They had many things in common, such as seeing light, grass, feeling an awesome power, hearing music. None, however, reported any signs of building and construction taking place.

In contrast, almost all reports that I have seen recorded and documented since 1960 include mention of builders constructing housing for a large number of people apparently expected to arrive at the same time. I believe it's about time for the coming of Christ our King to take us to our inherited home.

In 1960 my family was finally able to realize our dream of moving to Florida. My husband, daughter, and I along with my mother, dad, and two younger brothers, Marvin and Gary, had anticipated it for years, and now it was going to happen.

John and I sold our house and moved into a cramped little gray trailer with Brenda, her dog and cat, and forty dolls. We didn't mind being crowded. We were moving to Florida in a few weeks, as soon as the final paperwork was completed on selling my husband's business.

Someone whispered a rumor that we had lost our lovely ranch home and had to sell our business because of bankruptcy. We didn't even respond because we didn't really care. It didn't matter. We knew better. We were moving to Florida! And arriving in Florida was like going home.

We had nine wonderful years before both John and my mother died. I almost lost our home and had to move back to North Dakota with my two small children. But I told my neighbor, "I'll be back. This is home."

I left empty, but once again my dream came true and I came back full. I now have an honorable father for my children, a godly mate. Two years ago as we drove back across the Florida state line I felt my heart would burst with the homecoming.

Don't worry about ridicule from unbelievers as you prepare for the journey. Hold onto your dream. We're going home soon! The time for Jesus to come is sooner than it has ever been before.

You may feel burned out, battle-weary, battered, wounded, and discouraged. You may have climbed the ladder of success only to find it leaning against the wrong wall. You may be locked into a dead marriage or nursing a dream that has died or in pain with sickness. Then "look up, rejoice, for your redemption draweth nigh!" If we

stand in our shoes of hope on tiptoes of faith, we can see
the brightness of His glory. (See Ezekiel 1:28–2:1.)

We may be troubled on every side, yet we are not dis-
tressed. We are perplexed, but not in despair; persecuted,
but not forsaken; cast down, but not destroyed. We have
a treasure, the excellency of the power of God. And we
know that God who raised Jesus from the dead shall raise
us up, too! (See 2 Corinthians 4:6–18.)

An old Russian proverb says that "death takes not the
old, but the ripe." It has been harvest time for many.
Others may see (or feel!) the law of gravity fail in that
Rapture moment when "the trumpet will sound, and the
dead will be raised imperishable, and we shall be
changed" (1 Corinthians 15:52).

Are you what John Wesley described as an "almost
Christian" or are you a prepared bride, watching and
ready? "Let us rejoice and be glad and give the glory to
Him, for the marriage of the Lamb has come and His bride
has made herself ready" (Revelation 19:7).

Great events are about to occur, among the most interesting characteristics that time and eternity have ever
known. I believe our Lord has probably alerted the angelic
reception committees that the time has nearly arrived
when He shall leave the mediatorial throne and, in company with the saints and angels, descend to the earth. We
should tell it, write it, impress others with it. The "redemption of the purchased possession" is about to take
place. In a short while we will join in singing the song of
the Lamb.

If I die before Jesus comes, don't impose on a church
friend to whine through a mournful song at my funeral.
Put on John Hall's tape "Buried Alive" and listen with a

smile. One time John Hall and I were on the same television program. I got up out of the makeup chair, flung the apron off my chest, and rushed to the door of the television studio in time to hear him say, "The next verse I'm singing for Betty Malz." How thrilling it was to hear those joyful words: "When they lower these bones down in the ground, I'll be living on the other side!"

The other song I want sung at my funeral is on the tape my lovely friend Lillie Knauls sings: "Finally Home." "But just think of stepping on shore and finding it heaven! . . . Oh, of waking up in Glory, and finding you are home!"

It's no wonder our children, this generation, have become confused and frustrated. We keep forgetting to tell them that Jesus is coming again. That's good news!

My brother Marvin and his wife, Sharon, were sweethearts from the time they were children about ten years old. I shall always remember their Christmas wedding— and the days leading up to it. Marvin was in Florida and his fiancée in Indiana. He would write and phone to keep in touch. He bought a little four-room house for $5,000 that Mother and I helped him decorate and furnish in Sharon's then-favorite colors of blue and happy orange.

Finally, after the wedding in Indiana, the weariness of the two long days of travel vanished from their eyes when he parked in the shell driveway under two little palms he had planted. When he carried her across that humble threshold, they were home.

We want to go home, and Jesus wants us to come. It won't be long. We mustn't get discouraged and stop waiting for our arrival in our heavenly home. We mustn't give in to the temptation to believe anything other than what the Bible teaches.

The first lie that Satan used thousands of years ago is the same and the last one he will use now. He told Eve, "Eat of this tree and you will be as God." New groups these days, particularly those in the New Age movement, are saying, "There is no heaven, no hell. We will just become wiser and better. We are becoming gods even now."

This worship of ourselves is the epitome of pride and idolatry. That egotism is sharply contrasted with the humility expressed in the legend Ed Schlossmacher told in a sermon recently.

Zaccheus took a walk early each morning. One day his wife decided to follow him and find out where he went. The journey led her to the edge of town to a tree near the road. The tree was old, and Zaccheus bent and watered it, patted the trunk, hugged that old tree with loving, tender respect.

Why did he nourish that old tree? It was the place where Zaccheus found Jesus, eternal life, the hope of heaven.

Today go back in your memory to the place where He became life to you. Nothing should get in the way of our love for Him. Hardships in this life are only temporary. Take courage and remember that as soldiers of the cross we aren't looking for mansions on the battlefield. A tent will do. We are more concerned with getting the war over and going home.

A few years ago Mary Pallesen came over for a cup of tea. We sat on the sun deck overlooking the Red River Valley area of the prairies of the Dakotas and decided to walk out to Clark's Corner. We didn't contemplate the fact that it was eight miles out—and the same distance back! I made the mistake of wearing a $4 bargain pair of canvas deck shoes without socks. Her gear wasn't much better. We laughed when Carl suggested we not start out on our first walk with such a big goal, and somehow we actually arrived at Clark's Corner in pretty good repair. Then we turned for home.

There is not much traffic up there on the ridge. We prayed someone would come and pick us up; no one came. The last mile we were sliding our feet along the ground, dragging them in order to move. My left hip felt out of place, my back hurt, we were dehydrated, nearly faint, and my heels had bled so much my shoes were red in the back.

But our pride would not let us quit and our silly sense of humor volleyed back and forth encouraging us to make it. Suddenly we caught sight of the old brown farmhouse with the white gingerbread trim and windowboxes blooming with pink and white petunias! We had made it home! We had succeeded in our venture! We smiled ridiculously between long, gasping drinks of water and collapsed into chairs.

If we took the happiness we felt at that moment of homecoming and magnified it a million times it still could not compare with the exhilaration each of us will feel upon entering the gates of heaven. It seems too good to be true—but it is!

What a homecoming awaits us!

I'll see you at the banquet.